ICNS 2020

The Sixteenth International Conference on Networking and Services

September 27th – October 1st, 2020

ICNS 2020 Editors

Eugen Borcoci, University POLITEHNICA Bucharest, Romania

Mary Luz Mouronte López, Universidad Francisco de Vitoria - Madrid, Spain

Printed from e-media with permission by:

Curran Associates, Inc.
57 Morehouse Lane
Red Hook, NY 12571

Some format issues inherent in the e-media version may also appear in this print version.

Printed with permission by Curran Associates, Inc. (2020)

International Academy, Research, and Industry Association (IARIA)
412 Derby Way
Wilmington, DE 19810

Phone: (408) 893-6407
Fax: (408) 527-6351

petre@iaria.org

Additional copies of this publication are available from:

Curran Associates, Inc.
57 Morehouse Lane
Red Hook, NY 12571 USA
Phone: 845-758-0400
Fax: 845-758-2633
Email: curran@proceedings.com
Web: www.proceedings.com

Table of Contents

ICNS 2020

Forward

The Sixteenth International Conference on Networking and Services (ICNS 2020) continued a series of events targeting general networking and services aspects in multi-technologies environments. Ubiquitous services, next generation networks, inter-provider quality of service, GRID networks and services, and emergency services and disaster recovery were also considered.

IPv6, the Next Generation of the Internet Protocol, has seen over the past years tremendous activity related to its development, implementation and deployment. Its importance is unequivocally recognized by research organizations, businesses and governments worldwide. To maintain global competitiveness, governments are mandating, encouraging or actively supporting the adoption of IPv6 to prepare their respective economies for the future communication infrastructures. In the United States, government's plans to migrate to IPv6 has stimulated significant interest in the technology and accelerated the adoption process. Business organizations are also increasingly mindful of the IPv4 address space depletion and see within IPv6 a way to solve pressing technical problems. At the same time, the IPv6 technology continues to evolve beyond IPv4 capabilities. Communications equipment manufacturers and applications developers are actively integrating IPv6 in their products based on market demands.

IPv6 creates opportunities for new and more scalable IP based services while representing a fertile and growing area of research and technology innovation. The efforts of successful research projects, progressive service providers deploying IPv6 services and enterprises led to a significant body of knowledge and expertise. It is the goal of this workshop to facilitate the dissemination and exchange of technology and deployment related information, to provide a forum where academia and industry can share ideas and experiences in this field that could accelerate the adoption of IPv6. The workshop brings together IPv6 research and deployment experts that will share their work. The audience will hear the latest technological updates and will be provided with examples of successful IPv6 deployments; it will be offered an opportunity to learn what to expect from IPv6 and how to prepare for it.

Packet Dynamics refers broadly to measurements, theory and/or models that describe the time evolution and the associated attributes of packets, flows or streams of packets in a network. Factors impacting packet dynamics include cross traffic, architectures of intermediate nodes (e.g., routers, gateways, and firewalls), complex interaction of hardware resources and protocols at various levels, as well as implementations that often involve competing and conflicting requirements.

Parameters such as packet reordering, delay, jitter and loss that characterize the delivery of packet streams are at times highly correlated. Load-balancing at an intermediate node may, for example, result in out-of-order arrivals and excessive jitter, and network congestion may manifest as packet losses or large jitter. Out-of-order arrivals, losses, and jitter in turn may lead to unnecessary retransmissions in TCP or loss of voice quality in VoIP.

With the growth of the Internet in size, speed and traffic volume, understanding the impact of underlying network resources and protocols on packet delivery and application performance has assumed a critical importance. Measurements and models explaining the variation and interdependence of delivery characteristics are crucial not only for efficient operation of networks and network diagnosis, but also for developing solutions for future networks.

Local and global scheduling and heavy resource sharing are main features carried by Grid networks. Grids offer a uniform interface to a distributed collection of heterogeneous computational, storage and network resources. Most current operational Grids are dedicated to a limited set of computationally and/or data intensive scientific problems.

Optical burst switching enables these features while offering the necessary network flexibility demanded by future Grid applications. Currently ongoing research and achievements refers to high performance and computability in Grid networks. However, the communication and computation mechanisms for Grid applications require further development, deployment and validation.

We take here the opportunity to warmly thank all the members of the ICNS 2020 technical program committee, as well as all the reviewers. The creation of such a high quality conference program would not have been possible without their involvement. We also kindly thank all the authors who dedicated much of their time and effort to contribute to ICNS 2020. We truly believe that, thanks to all these efforts, the final conference program consisted of top quality contributions. We also thank the members of the ICNS 2020 organizing committee for their help in handling the logistics of this event.

ICNS 2020 Chairs

ICNS 2020 Steering Committee

Eugen Borcoci, University "Politehnica" of Bucharest (UPB), Romania
Mary Luz Mouronte López, Universidad Francisco de Vitoria – Madrid, Spain
Carlos Becker Westphall, Federal University of Santa Catarina, Brazil
Jeff Sedayao, Intel Corporation, USA
Alex Sim, Lawrence Berkeley National Laboratory, USA
Juraj Giertl, T-Systems, Slovakia
Ivan Ganchev, University of Limerick, Ireland, Plovdiv University "Paisii Hilendarski", Bulgaria

ICNS 2020 Publicity Chair

Joseyda Jaqueline More, Universitat Politecnica de Valencia, Spain
Marta Botella-Campos, Universitat Politecnica de Valencia, Spain

ICNS 2020 Industry/Research Advisory Committee

Steffen Fries, Siemens, Germany
Sathiamoorthy Manoharan, University of Auckland, New Zealand
Massimo Villari, Universita' di Messina, Italy
Éric Renault, Institut Mines-Télécom - Télécom SudParis, France
Young-Joo Suh, POSTECH (Pohang University of Science and Technology), Korea

Rui L.A. Aguiar, University of Aveiro, Portugal

ICNS 2020
Committee

ICNS 2020 Steering Committee
Eugen Borcoci, University "Politehnica" of Bucharest (UPB), Romania
Mary Luz Mouronte López, Universidad Francisco de Vitoria – Madrid, Spain
Carlos Becker Westphall, Federal University of Santa Catarina, Brazil
Jeff Sedayao, Intel Corporation, USA
Alex Sim, Lawrence Berkeley National Laboratory, USA
Juraj Giertl, T-Systems, Slovakia
Ivan Ganchev, University of Limerick, Ireland, Plovdiv University "Paisii Hilendarski", Bulgaria

ICNS 2020 Publicity Chair
Joseyda Jaqueline More, Universitat Politecnica de Valencia, Spain
Marta Botella-Campos, Universitat Politecnica de Valencia, Spain

ICNS 2020 Industry/Research Advisory Committee
Steffen Fries, Siemens, Germany
Sathiamoorthy Manoharan, University of Auckland, New Zealand
Massimo Villari, Universita' di Messina, Italy
Éric Renault, Institut Mines-Télécom - Télécom SudParis, France
Young-Joo Suh, POSTECH (Pohang University of Science and Technology), Korea
Rui L.A. Aguiar, University of Aveiro, Portugal

ICNS 2020 Technical Program Committee
Abdelhafid Abouaissa, University of Haute-Alsace, France
Fatemah Alharbi, University of California, Riverside, USA / Taibah University, Yanbu, Saudi Arabia
Adel Alshamrani, University of Jeddah, Saudi Arabia
Delaram Amiri, University of California Irvine, USA
Patrick Appiah-Kubi, University of Maryland University College, USA
Michael Atighetchi, Raytheon BBN Technologies, USA
Muhammed Ali Aydin, Istanbul University - Cerrahpaşa, Turkey
Bharath Balasubramanian, ATT Labs Research, USA
Mohammad M. Banat, Jordan University of Science and Technology, Jordan
Ilija Basicevic, University of Novi Sad, Serbia
Robert Bestak, Czech Technical University in Prague, Czech Republic
Hasan Burhan Beytur, Middle East Technical University, Turkey
Eugen Borcoci, University "Politehnica" of Bucharest (UPB), Romania
Fernando Boronat Seguí, Universidad Politécnica De Valencia-Campus De Gandia, Spain
Abdelmadjid Bouabdallah, Université de Technologie de Compiègne (UTC), France
Christos Bouras, University of Patras / Computer Technology Institute and Press - Diophantus, Greece
An Braeken, Vrije Universiteit Brussels (VUB), Belgium
Maria-Dolores Cano, Universidad Politécnica de Cartagena, Spain
José Cecílio, University of Coimbra, Portugal
Subhrendu Chattopadhyay, Indian Institute of Technology Guwahati, Assam, India
Hao Che, University of Texas at Arlington, USA

Copyright Information

GuideMe: A Networked Application for Indoor Orientation and Guidance

Eirini Barri
Department of Computer Engineering and Informatics
University of Patras
Patras, Greece
e-mail: ebarri@ceid.upatras.gr

Christos Bouras
Department of Computer Engineering and Informatics
University of Patras
Patras, Greece
e-mail: bouras@cti.gr

Apostolos Gkamas
University Ecclesiastical Academy of Vella
Ioannina, Greece
e-mail: gkamas@aeavellas.gr

Christina Koulouri
Department of Computer Engineering and Informatics
University of Patras
Patras, Greece
e-mail: christinakoul1995@hotmail.gr

Evangelos Michos
Department of Computer Engineering and Informatics
University of Patras
Patras, Greece
e-mail: emichos@ceid.upatras.gr

Spyridon Aniceto Katsampiris Salgado
Department of Computer Engineering and Informatics
University of Patras
Patras, Greece
e-mail: ksalgado@ceid.upatras.gr

Abstract—**Today's indoor navigational systems are more and more in demand, commonly used for applications such as smart cities, robots and visually impaired people. As far as outdoor navigation is concerned, the Global Positioning System (GPS) technology is still one of the most (if not the most) commonly used approaches. Even though it is still considered an ideal solution for navigating in outdoor areas, challenges and problems arise when GPS is considered for navigation inside buildings due to obstacles (e.g., shopping malls, hospitals, etc.) and because signals cannot be absorbed by the building walls. To tackle the aforementioned issue, other technologies have emerged aimed at indoor navigation, such as Wireless-Fidelity (Wi-Fi), Bluetooth and sensors. This paper's contribution is towards indoor navigation and, more specifically, it targets designing and developing a tracking and navigation system aimed at people that experience difficulties in indoor orientation using a wearable device. The user takes direction from the wearable device for the indoor orientation through voice commands helping him to avoid obstacles. The central part of the system is a device that provides the ability to navigate and find a route by voice commands, based on the device's location and orientation capabilities.**

Keywords-GuideMe; indoor navigation; trilateration; pathfinding; UWB; BLE: people with special needs.

I. INTRODUCTION

Undoubtedly, there is an increasing demand for efficient indoor navigation systems, demand that mainly derives from smart cities, robots and visually impaired people, only to name a few. As far as outdoor navigation and pathfinding are concerned, the Global Positioning System (GPS) is still considered among the most commonly used technologies. Yet, this is only efficiently applicable in outdoor locations, because when indoor navigation comes into play, issues do rise. Of course, indoor navigation is very important to us and has many applications for humans and robots. Two of the most common issues that arise are a) the fact that physical obstacles inside building cannot be labeled as obstacles from the GPS and b) the fact that signals cannot be absorbed by walls inside buildings. Multiple floors, rooms and obstacles inside each and every indoor area pose a major problem. Additionally, the inability to use the GPS technology inside buildings makes indoor navigation more complicated, for reasons already explained above [1].

On the good side, many recent studies have been and are still conducted in order to make indoor navigation more effective and efficient. The direct need for new applications and technologies that can efficiently tackle such issues can luckily be covered by other available indoor navigation technologies that do exist nowadays, such as Wireless-Fidelity (Wi-Fi), Bluetooth and sensors.

This paper provides the design and development of a tracking and navigation system for people with special needs for indoor locations. In its core, the system consists of a device that provides the ability to navigate and route by voice commands, based on the device's location and orientation capabilities. This device shall be connected to the server via the user's mobile phone (android). The overall system (when completed) will consist of the following components:

- Equipment permanently installed in selected areas.
- A cloud server that will synchronize and coordinate the various parts, store information about the facilities and users, and will be responsible for the accounting and invoicing parts.
- Portable devices.
- Software that will run on smartphones.

The rest of this paper is organized as follows. Section II describes the motivation behind our work. Section III provides a literature review of other current works on this subject. Section IV addresses the system's architecture whereas Section V goes into finer details in regard to the proposed algorithms for positioning and navigating in indoor spaces. Finally, Section VI summarizes our main findings and conclusions and suggests probable future work. The acknowledgement and conclusions close the article.

II. Motivation

Blindness is the condition of lacking visual perception due to physiological or neurological factors. Blind people face many problems in everyday life. They always depend on others. They cannot move easily from one place to another without help from others.

According to the World Health Organization, the following are the key facts regarding blindness and vision impairment [2]:

- Globally, at least 2.2 billion people have a vision impairment or blindness, of whom at least 1 billion have a vision impairment that could have been prevented or has yet to be addressed.
- This 1 billion people include those with moderate or severe distance vision impairment or blindness due to unaddressed refractive error, as well as near vision impairment caused by unaddressed presbyopia.
- Globally, the leading causes of vision impairment are uncorrected refractive errors and cataracts.
- The majority of people with vision impairment are over the age of 50 years.

The motivation of the GuideMe project [3] is to provide guidance and security for out-of-home travel. The central part of the system is a portable device that provides the ability to route and navigate by voice commands. The instructions will be based on the device's location and orientation capabilities. The device will be connected to the server via the user's mobile phone. The solution is built around a discreet portable device capable of indoor localization with an accuracy of 10 cm using Ultra-wideband (UWB) technology. The device can also determine the orientation, receive voice commands, and transmit voice instructions.

The motivation of the paper is to improve two areas of social life of the blind people and people with special needs in general: convenience and security. Specifically, with the use of the proposed system, users will feel more comfortable visiting public places, such as airports, shopping malls, stations, etc. as they will be guided by the system to reach their destination. At the same time, in case of emergencies involving both the user (accidents) and the building (fire, earthquake, etc.), the system will inform the users of the exact location of the users, whilst also guiding them to the nearest exit. The ultimate goal is to increase the presence of the population with mobility or other problems in buildings by 20%.

III. Related Work

There are several studies concerning indoor positioning techniques and systems. Previous works focus on the need to study the general way of positioning and then they propose algorithms and methods for indoor positioning. Daramouskas et al. [4] study methods for location estimation on Low Power Wide Area Networks (LPWAN). They also present Multilateration, Trilateration and Particle Swarm Optimization (PSO) algorithm, according to previous research, which constitute the three most commonly used methods to calculate the location of a moving object, based on distance measurements. Choliz et al. [5], gather all existing algorithms for UWB positioning and tracking systems and evaluate the performance in a realistic interior scenario. Next, Krishnaveni et al. [6] present an overview of indoor positioning based on UWB technology.

In the literature on positioning, machine learning algorithms are widely used to estimate position. Some of the machine learning algorithms used in indoor positioning are presented in [7]. Liu et al. [8], present a summary table with a comparison of recent systems and provide solutions about current wireless indoor positioning systems. A survey of the latest indoor positioning technologies is provided by Alarifi et al. [9], who analyze UWB technologies with an analysis of Strengths, Weaknesses, Opportunities, and Threats (SWOT). Unlike previous studies, Al-Ammar et al. [10] present new taxonomies and review some major recent advances on indoor positioning techniques. Finally, in [11], Mahida et al. deal with various positioning enabled wireless technologies and algorithms used in realistic scenarios to provide indoor navigation.

As far as indoor navigation is concerned, there exists a variety of significant work for people with special needs. More specifically, giving emphasis in works of the last years, we have found several similar approaches. Kishore et al. [12] provided a comprehensive solution for indoor public transport for people with disabilities. Beacons (small low-power devices, which are increasingly gaining recognition and application in malls and airports) were placed indoors and transmitted signals to the cell phone sensors via Bluetooth Low Energy (BLE) technology. Cheraghi et al. [13], BLE beacons-based indoor navigation was developed under the name GuideBeacon, where simulations showed that the GuideBeacon application reduces the time it takes for a disabled person to cross an unknown indoor area by 30%-50% and reduced the required distance they have to walk by at least 50%. Link et al. [14] suggested a system called FootPath, which obtains a geographic map from OpenStreetMap. After downloading the geographic map, the system uses the accelerometer and compass on the user's phone to calculate and detect the user's steps. The results showed that the FootPath system is very accurate to assist users with disabilities and indoors.

Megalingam et al. [15], proposed a system to find the best route for wheelchair users based on minimal changes in direction. The algorithm suggested is called Location-Aware and Remembering Navigation (LARN) and it depends on Dijkstra's algorithm to find the optimal path. The study carried out in [16] introduced a new method for dynamically changing the navigation path indoors. The proposed algorithm was named FPP and combined its internal path information and interior information. The FPP algorithm was compared with those of Dijkstra and Elastic and the results showed that FPP can provide the shortest route for in-house navigation faster than the other two algorithms. Goel, et al. [17], studied indoor navigation in order to reduce the time required for a user to get to its destination, using algorithm A*. The first section of the paper was devoted to a detailed presentation of A* algorithm, while in the second one, the authors successfully demonstrated why the A* algorithm is better than Dijkstra algorithm for indoor navigation with barriers. Comparing A* and Dijkstra for indoor navigation, A* achieves better results through heuristic searches and delivers better results faster.

Following the previous studies, in this section we will present similar projects to GuideMe. Indoo.rs and San Francisco International Airport worked together to create an app for visually impaired passengers. The Entrepreneurship-in-Residence (EIR) project is an Edwin M. Lee collaboration with the White House and other San Francisco business partners. At the beginning of 2014, they chose to help the San Francisco Airport (SFO) create a tool to assist blind and visually impaired travelers [18]. Recommendation ITU-T F.921 [19] sets out how audio-based network navigation systems can be designed to ensure that they are dedicated and responsive to the needs of people with visual impairments. The aim is to provide network visual system designers with the audio data they need in the early stages of development to anticipate and overcome any constraints and obstacles that prevent vision impaired users from making full use of the built environment. The purpose of [20] was to implement a module-based application developed in the context of preliminary projects for the mobile mass market. Through an appropriate user interface that responds to the needs of the visually impaired, the blind user should be able to use public transport independently in a secure manner and navigate complex public transport terminals. The system combines real-time communication to and from public transport vehicles with precise positioning and guidance while it also provides additional navigation assistance.

INK 2016: Indoor Navigation and Communication in ÖPNV for blind and visually impaired people [21] combines real-time communication to and from public transport vehicles with precise positioning and guidance and has additional video call navigation assistance where the person can communicate with a professional operator. Arikovani UK's WeWalk, Imperial College London, Astra Terra and the Royal National Institute of Blind People (RNIB) will cooperate to mitigate indoor wayfinding challenges by developing an indoor navigation system that is both reliable and fully accessible for visually impaired people and anyone that may struggle to navigate the built environment [22]. Project Ways4all [23] is a new personalized indoor navigation system that can increase public transport accessibility for all passengers and especially the visually impaired, who will be able to access public transport and the necessary up-to-date traffic information in a very simplified way. Finally, Project "Using An Integrated Techniques for Developing Indoor Navigation Systems to Allow the Blind and Visually Impaired People to Reach Precise Objects" [24] uses a set of different technologies (WIFI, Bluetooth, and RFID) to help the user reach a micro element in the navigated environment. It constitutes an intelligent interface for precise indoor navigation for blind and visually impaired people using a smart phone.

IV. System Architecture

In this project, the main component is a small wearable that helps in the user's positioning through UWB technology. This technology provides very accurate positioning, up to 10 cm divergence. This device, apart from the ability to locate the user, can also determine the orientation of the user, receive voice commands, and transmit voice instructions to guide the visually impaired people.

Specifically, as it is shown in Figure 1, in our proposed system, our smart device can communicate to anchors via UWB technology, in order to locate the user. This device has the ability to provide route and navigation information to the user via voice commands. The anchors are calculating and measuring the distance between the user and the anchor. The distance data (between the user and the anchors), is transferred to a local server in order to measure the exact position and run positioning algorithms, that in our case will be trilateration. The positioning algorithms are described in the Section V. Furthermore, there is a remote server that has a map of the building. This remote server, having the details of the building and the position of the user and the destination of the user, can provide guidance to the user by giving directions. The directions are given by the smartphone to the user through wireless headphones, using voice commands.

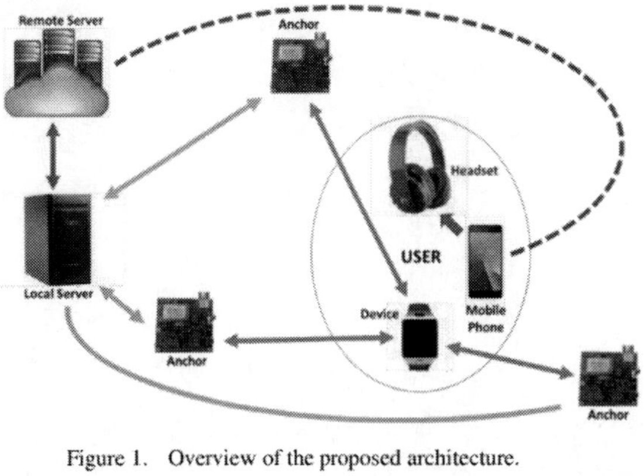

Figure 1. Overview of the proposed architecture.

As far as the wearable device is concerned, the processor that is chosen is the module made by Econais, the EC32L13 [25]. The EC32L13 is a 32-bit processor of the product family STM32 processors. This processors in this family of processors are energy efficient, in order to expand the battery life. A WiFi module is also integrated into the wearable device. For the connectivity through UWB, we have chosen the module DWM1000 of Decawave.

In Figure 2, we present the general architecture of the wearable device. The device consists of some sensors such as, the magnetometer and accelerometer sensors, the UWB module, the WiFi module, the Main Computing Unit, which in our case is the EC32L13 and module for the battery management as well, in order to expand the battery life as long as possible.

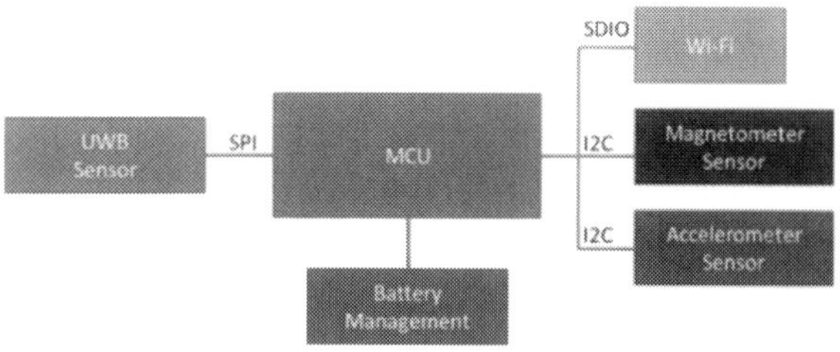

Figure 2. Overview of the device's architecture.

V. PROPOSED ALGORITHMS

In this section, we will present our indoor positioning algorithms and the indoor navigation algorithm we used and integrated in our system.

A. Indoor Positioning

As far as indoor positioning is concerned, as part of the GuideMe project, it was decided to implement the trilateration algorithm that combines simple implementation and sufficiently precise positioning beyond the project requirements.

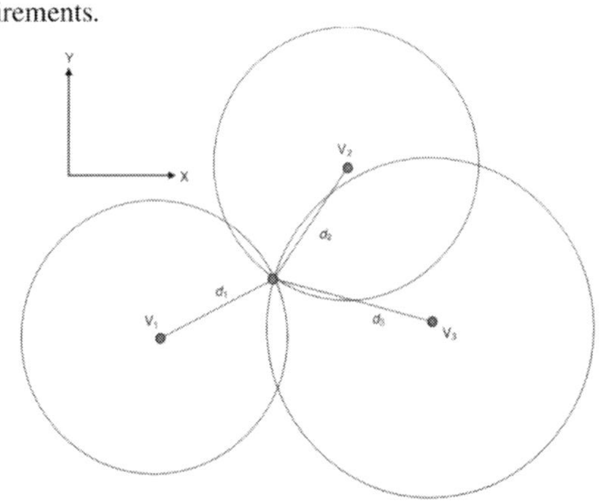

Figure 3. Represenation of trilateration.

The trilateration algorithm is a fairly common and easy to understand algorithm and is used extensively in various applications. Also, the DW 1000 module used in the project supports Time Difference of Arrival (TDoA), a method that gives a very good distance estimation. The high data rate and speed of the UWB can reach 100 Megabits per second (Mbps), which makes it a good solution for indoor positioning. Thus, the trilateration algorithm can give a very good estimate of the user's position. The logic that is followed is: for each anchor the user communicates with, a circle is created with its center being the position of the user and the radius the distance between the user and the anchor. This should be done for at least 3 anchors. The point where the circles intersect is the location of the user. Before we begin the description of the implementation and the code, we give an image describing the three cases considered in the trilateration method, in Figure 3. In Algorithm 1, our approach of the localization of the user is described.

Algorithm 1: Trilateration Algorithm for indoor positioning

```
Class circle(point,radius){
  this.point=point;
}
function Locate(x1, y1,distance1, x2, y2,distance2, x3, y3,distance3){
  create circle objects;
  circle_list={c1,c2,c3}
  get_all_intersecting_points(circle_list);
  center=Get_center_of_polygon(intersected_points_list);
}
function get_all_intersecting_points(circle_list){
  //intersecting points of every circle with the other circles
  find_interecting_points_by_two_circle(circle(i), circle(k));
}
function get_polygon_center(points){
    center = point(0, 0);
    num = len(points)
    for i in range(num){
      center.x += points[i].x
      center.y += points[i].y
    }
    return center
}
```

B. Indoor Navigation

For the needs of the project, it was decided to use Algorithm A* for indoor navigation (based on [16], Algorithm A* is an optimal algorithm for indoor routing). Algorithm A* is a pathfinding algorithm that is widely used because of its completeness and optimum efficiency. In systems where navigation through barrier is required, A* is still the best solution for the majority of cases. This algorithm is based on structured graphs. It defines an initial node of the graph as a start node and attempts to find the path to the final node at minimum cost. The minimum cost does not necessarily have to do with the minimum number of moves, as it could e.g., UWB indicates the shortest path length.

To implement the algorithm, a path tree is constructed that starts from the start node and extends the tree paths, one edge at a time, until the algorithm termination criterion is met. At each iteration, the set of paths to be expanded must be specified, and to do so, the travel cost is used in conjunction with an estimate of the costs required to extend to the final node. Therefore, the algorithm will select that path that minimizes:

$$f(n) = g(n) + h(n) \tag{1}$$

where n is the next extension node in the graph, g(n) is the path cost from the original node to n and g(n) the cost of the minimum cost from the extension node n to the terminal node. The algorithm terminates when an acceptable extension is found from the start node to the terminal node, otherwise extensions to the node are not available. As for the efficiency of A*, as long as this algorithm never overestimates the actual cost to reach the terminal, then the returned path will always be of minimal cost.

At the programming level of the algorithm, the Javascript library Easystar.js will be used [26]. Based on this library, we will first need to set a grid where the accepted values will be 0 or 1, depending on which cells are accessible and which are not (the matching can be done as we wish). Having defined which cells are accessible, by defining the (x,y) start and stop coordinate pairs, the path of algorithm A* can be calculated, if it exists.

The pseudocode of algorithm A* is presented below (we accept the Wikipedia approach for the algorithm [27]):

Algorithm 2: A* Algorithm for Indoor Navigation

```
begin
function reconstruct_path(cameFrom, current)
  total_path := {current}
  while current in cameFrom.keys:
    current := cameFrom[current]
    total_path.prepend(current)
  return total_path
function A_Star(start, goal, h)
  openSet := {start}
  cameFrom := an empty map
  gScore := map with default value of Infinity
  gScore[start] := 0
  fScore := map with default value of Infinity
  fScore[start] := h(start)
  while openSet is not empty
    current := the node in openSet having the lowest fScore[] value
    if current = goal
      return reconstruct_path(cameFrom, current)
    openSet.Remove(current)
    for each neighbor of current
      tentative_gScore := gScore[current] + d(current, neighbor)
      if tentative_gScore < gScore[neighbor]
        cameFrom[neighbor] := current
        gScore[neighbor] := tentative_gScore
        fScore[neighbor] := gScore[neighbor] + h(neighbor)
        if neighbor not in openSet
          openSet.add(neighbor)
  return failure
end
```

VI. Conclusion and Future Work

This work refers to the project of GuideMe. The state of the art of existing approaches and the algorithms that were implemented to complete the project in terms of navigation and indoor routing were presented. By providing a wearable device, the project is contributing to indoor navigation and positioning assistance for people with difficulties. The user takes direction from the wearable device for the indoor orientation through voice commands that help with avoiding obstacles. This work is the basis of the next step of the project that relates to transmitting the correct instructions to the user using the information of the algorithms of the position of the mobile device as well as the path to follow through voice commands. Future work may include an extension of this current work by also covering outdoor areas through the application.

Acknowledgment

This research has been co-financed by the European Union and Greek national funds through the Regional Operation Program "Western Greece 2014-2020", under the Call "Regional research and innovation strategies for smart specialization (RIS3) in Communication and Information Technologies" (project code: 5038620 entitled "System for indoors orientation and guidance - GuideMe").

References

[1] E. J. Alqahtani, F. H. Alshamrani, H. F. Syed and F. A. Alhaidari, "Survey on Algorithms and Techniques for Indoor Navigation Systems," 21st Saudi Computer Society National Computer Conference (NCC), Riyadh, 2018, pp. 1-9.

[2] https://www.who.int/news-room/fact-sheets/detail/blindness-and-visual-impairment 2019.12.11.

[3] http://www.guideme-project.upatras.gr/ 2019.12.11.

[4] I. Daramouskas, V. Kapoulas and T. Pegiazis, "A survey of methods for location estimation on Low Power Wide Area Networks," 10th International Conference on Information, Intelligence, Systems and Applications (IISA), Patras, Greece, 2019, pp. 1-4, doi: 10.1109/IISA.2019.8900701.

[5] J. Choliz, M. Eguizabal, A. Hernandez-Solana and A. Valdovinos, "Comparison of Algorithms for UWB Indoor Location and Tracking Systems," IEEE 73rd Vehicular Technology Conference (VTC Spring), Yokohama, 2011, pp. 1-5, doi: 10.1109/VETECS.2011.5956174.

[6] B. V. Krishnaveni, K. S.Reddy and P. R. Reddy, "Ultra Wideband Indoor Positioning Technologies: Analysis and Recent Advances," Sensors, vol. 16, no. 5, May 2016, pp. 707, doi: 10.3390/s16050707.

[7] S. Bozkurt, G. Elibol, S. Gunal, and U. Yayan, "A comparative study on machine learning algorithms for indoor positioning," International Symposium on Innovations in Intelligent SysTems and Applications (INISTA), Sep. 2015, doi: 10.1109/inista.2015.7276725.

[8] H. Liu, H. Darabi, P. Banerjee and J. Liu, "Survey of Wireless Indoor Positioning Techniques and Systems," in IEEE

Transactions on Systems, Man, and Cybernetics, Part C (Applications and Reviews), vol. 37, no. 6, pp. 1067-1080, Nov. 2007, doi: 10.1109/TSMCC.2007.905750.

[9] A. Alarifi et al., "Ultra Wideband Indoor Positioning Technologies: Analysis and Recent Advances," Sensors, vol. 16, no. 5, p. 707, May 2016, doi: 10.3390/s16050707.

[10] M. A. Al-Ammar et al., "Comparative Survey of Indoor Positioning Technologies, Techniques, and Algorithms," International Conference on Cyberworlds, Santander, 2014, pp. 245-252, doi: 10.1109/CW.2014.41.

[11] P. T. Mahida, S. Shahrestani and H. Cheung, "Localization techniques in indoor navigation system for visually impaired people," 17th International Symposium on Communications and Information Technologies (ISCIT), Cairns, QLD, 2017, pp. 1-6, doi: 10.1109/ISCIT.2017.8261229.

[12] A. Kishore et al., "CENSE: A Cognitive Navigation System for People with Special Needs," IEEE Third International Conference on Big Data Computing Service and Applications (BigDataService), San Francisco, CA, 2017, pp. 198-203, doi: 10.1109/BigDataService.2017.32.

[13] S. A. Cheraghi, V. Namboodiri and L. Walker, "GuideBeacon: Beacon-based indoor wayfinding for the blind, visually impaired, and disoriented," 2017 IEEE International Conference on Pervasive Computing and Communications (PerCom), Kona, HI, 2017, pp. 121-130, doi: 10.1109/PERCOM.2017.7917858.

[14] J. Á. B. Link, P. Smith, N. Viol and K. Wehrle, "FootPath: Accurate map-based indoor navigation using smartphones," International Conference on Indoor Positioning and Indoor Navigation, Guimaraes, 2011, pp. 1-8, doi: 10.1109/IPIN.2011.6071934.

[15] R. K. Megalingam, A. P. Rajendran, D. Dileepkumar and A. T. Soloman, "LARN: Indoor navigation for elderly and physically challenged," IEEE Global Humanitarian Technology Conference (GHTC), San Jose, CA, 2013, pp. 326-330, doi: 10.1109/GHTC.2013.6713705.

[16] Y. Li and B.-S. Shin, "Internal Topology Based Flexible Shortest Path Planning Method for Indoor Navigation," in Lecture Notes in Electrical Engineering, Springer Berlin Heidelberg, 2015, pp. 171–176, doi: https://doi.org/10.1007/978-3-662-47487-7_26.

[17] S. K. Goel, S. Ansari, and T. Kuwalekar, "Using A * algorithm to find shortest path in Indoor positioning system." 2017.

[18] https://indoo.rs/indoo-rs-and-san-francisco-international-airport-unveil-app-for-visually-impaired-passengers/ 2019.12.11.

[19] https://www.itu.int/rec/T-REC-F.921-201808-I/en

[20] https://trimis.ec.europa.eu/project/indoor-navigation-and-communication-public-transport-blind-and-visually-impaired 2019.12.11.

[21] https://www.tugraz.at/institute/ifg/projects/navigation/ink/ 2019.12.11.

[22] https://www.tdebproject.com/partnerships/mitigating-indoor-wayfinding-challenges 2019.12.11.

[23] http://www.ways4all.at/index.php/en/ways4all 2019.12.11.

[24] http://it.yu.edu.jo/index.php/it-faculty/facutly-projects/123-english-articles/242-using-an-integrated-techniques-for-developing-indoor-navigation-systems-to-allow-the-blind-and-visually-impaired-people-to-reach-precise-objects 2019.12.11.

[25] https://www.electronicsdatasheets.com/manufacturers/econais/parts/ec32l13 2019.12.11

[26] https://github.com/prettymuchbryce/easystarjs 2019.12.11.

[27] https://en.wikipedia.org/wiki/A*_search_algorithm 2019.12.11.

Resource Allocation Mechanism for Massive MIMO

Christos Bouras, Vasileios Kokkinos, Christina Koulouri
Computer Engineering and Informatics Department
University of Patras, Greece
Patras, Greece
e-mail: bouras@cti.gr, kokkinos@cti.gr, christinakoul1995@hotmail.com

***Abstract*—Nowadays, mobile users need faster data speeds and more reliable service. The next generation of wireless networks 5G pledges to commit that, and much more. Multiple-Input, Multiple-Output (MIMO) technology in 5G networks is studied in this paper, with emphasis on the achieved performance in terms of achieved Bandwidth. Multi-antenna technologies, such as MIMO, are anticipated to play a key role in 5G systems, as they will have to handle much higher speeds than today's cellular networks and greater network traffic. Specifically, we will refer to Massive MIMO (Ma-MIMO) technology. In this paper, a resource allocation mechanism is proposed from the Base Station (BS) to the available antennas, using the Knapsack Problem (KP) algorithm. Our goal is to evaluate user access throughput to the antennas and to study the case where the BS allocates resources, according to the channel rate it receives from each User Equipment (UE). The scenario executed is about serving the maximum number of UE connected to the BS, in high quality services. Finally, we simulate the results in MATLAB, in order to be able to evaluate the Quality of Service (QoS) that is provided to the UE by the BS, with the resource allocation technique that is proposed.**

Keywords-Massive MIMO; 5G; Knapsack Problem; wireless users; resource block.

I. Introduction

Some of the main reasons that lead us to the direction of 5G networks is the necessity for greater capacity, improved Data Rate (DR), decreased latency, massive device connectivity, lower cost and better Quality of Service (QoS) It is expected these days that around 2020, a new fifth generation of mobile networks (5G) is going to be developed. The 5G network is the next major generation of cellular mobile communications beyond the current 4G/IMT-Advanced standards. It is anticipated to maintain a significant quantity of mobile data traffic and a really big number of wireless connections to deliver better cost and energy efficiency, as well as QoS in respect of communication delay, reliability, and security. In order to achieve that, five brand-new technologies are designed, including millimeter waves, small cells, Massive MIMO (Ma-MIMO), full duplex, and beamforming.

With a primary adjust of the proper systems that refer to both communication and localization, location-aware communication can be perceived and a huge number of Location Based Services can be supported. 5G networks have a superior transmission scheme named Beam Division Multiple Access (BDMA). This technology serves simultaneously multiple User Equipment (UE) via different beams. Considering the communication between the Base Station (BS) and the UE, an orthogonal beam is dispensed to each mobile user. In this way, the capacity of the system is increased, owing to the BDMA technique that divides the antenna beam conforming to the UE position [1].

Ma-MIMO technology is a key enabler and foundational component when it comes to creating the next generation of network standards. MIMO stands for Multiple-input multiple-output. It is characterized by wireless systems, that allow to transmit and receive simultaneously more than one data signal over the same radio channel. This is accomplished by using separate antennas in the transmit and receive end for each data signal. In our days, 4G BSs have a dozen ports for antennas that handle all cellular traffic. From those twelve, eight of them are for transmitters and four for receivers. On the contrary, 5G BSs can support about a hundred ports, which signifies that on a single array many more antennas can fit.

In previous research work, a greedy–knapsack algorithm is proposed to analyze system performance. The authors of [2] evaluate UE that wait to be served. Then, they choose from a set of UE to maximize system performance in an optimal way, without exceeding the available bandwidth capacity in LTE networks. Other work like [3], remodel the number of transmit antennas as a Knapsack Problem (KP). Furthermore, the authors of [4] investigate the Signal-to-Interference-plus-Noise Ratio (*SINR)* precoding for Ma-MIMO systems, since they need to bring quality to a satisfactory level. Related work like [2][3][4], have explored the resource allocation technique using the KP formulation.

In this paper, a resource allocation mechanism from the BS to the available antennas is proposed, using the KP algorithm. This algorithm is a different approach of MIMO technology, as it seeks to serve as many UE as possible, with the support of a great service level. Our goal is to evaluate user access throughput to the antennas and to study the case where the BS allocates resources, according to the channel rate it receives from each antenna. The scenario described is about serving the maximum number of UE connected to the BS whereas some UE are on limits of a cell. It is very important for the proposed mechanism to manage to serve these UE, achieving a satisfying level of QoS, in terms of achieved Bandwidth. The resource allocation mechanism is proposed in a Ma-MIMO system. However, the results presented, are based on calculations, using a smaller number of users at every base station, in order to present the experiments effectively. Finally, we will simulate the proposed algorithm in MATLAB, in order to be able to evaluate if the UE's requests are served in an optimal way. To achieve this, we apply the 0-1 Knapsack Algorithm in our implementation. The variations in the number of UE connected to the BS, interference and other simulation parameters, will also be analyzed.

The rest of this paper is organized as follows. Section II provides a thorough analysis of the System Model in Ma-MIMO. Section III provides the proposed mechanism for the resource allocation. Section IV provides the simulation setup for our scenario. In Section V, we display and discuss the results from the simulation that evaluate our system model. Finally, in Section VI, we state our summarized conclusion for this paper and provide insights for future work.

II. SYSTEM MODEL

MIMO is an antenna technology for wireless communication that uses multiple transmission and receiving antennas. The antennas at the source and the destination are unified to reduce errors and optimize data speed [5]. This technology offers enormous advantages with respect to energy efficiency, spectral efficiency, robustness and reliability [6]. MIMO specifically attributes to a practical technique for sending and receiving more than one data signal simultaneously over the same radio channel taking advantage of multipath propagation. In practice, the channel between the transmitter and receiver is estimated from orthogonal pilot sequences, which are limited by the coherence time of the channel [7].

Concerning Ma-MIMO technology, the term has been produced for using a much larger number of antennas per location. As reported by the authors of [6], the main idea is to use large antenna arrays at the BS to simultaneously serve many autonomous terminals. Ma-MIMO technology relies on a plain processing of signals from all the antennas at BS. Therefore, with more ports for antennas the BS can serve more UE at the same time and obtain better beamforming. This greatly improves the BS's capacity and range. Still, using antenna panels covering 360 °, the classic antenna boundary problems can be avoided, since the BS (Ma-MIMO) can thus be adapted in the optimal way to the UE's movement in different directions. Moreover, the antenna arrays can be located in different positions at each BS, which then allows for optimal transmission of signals from different antenna locations.

As pointed out by the authors of [8][9] and the authors of [10] consider a Ma-MIMO network with K links using the same time–frequency resource, ending up in co-channel interference. Therefore, the target link k receives data that constitute an additive combination of required signal, interference, and noise. They use scalars x_k to declare the transmitted signals by the k-th link's transmitter and they depicted the received signal, y_k, at user k, as:

$$y_k = r_k^+ H_{k,k}^+ t_k x_k + \sum_{i=1, i \neq k}^{K} r_k^+ H_{k,i}^+ t_i x_i + r_k^+ n_k \quad (1)$$

where t_k represents the $M \times 1$ precoding vector and r_k is a $N \times 1$ beamforming vector. Finally, n_k represents the Gaussian noise vector at the receiver, while $H_{k,i}$ is the $M \times N$ channel state matrix from receiver k to transmitter i.

More research has been done in order to achieve a better resource allocation regarding the DownLink (DL) network. In [2], a greedy–knapsack algorithm is presented to estimate UE, which are waiting for scheduling. Then, they choose an optimal set of UE in order to maximize the performance of the system. Certainly, this needs to be done without exceeding the disposable bandwidth capacity in LTE networks. Furthermore, as presented in [3], so as to produce a service with an achievable quality, the number of the antennas at the source required, is determined by modifying it as a KP. Also, the BS transmits a signal vector with beamforming and is clarified in [3]. Moreover, in [4] the authors express the receiving signal of user k in cell j, as well as the *DL SINR* in a Ma-MIMO system and according to them, the DL *SINR* of user k in cell j is expressed as:

$$SINR_{j,k} = \frac{\left|f_{jk}^{j} \, a_{jk}\right| 2}{1 + \sum_{i=1, i \neq j}^{I} \sum_{k=1}^{K} \left|f_{jk}^{j} \, a_{jk}\right| 2} \quad (2)$$

where q_{ik} is DL transmission signals and $I = E\,[q_{ik}\, q_{ik}^{H}]$. Also, a_{jk} is the precoding matrix and f_{jk}^{j} is the channel matrix from the base station of cell j to UE k of cell j. Based on the research of the above authors, we will present an optimal Knapsack algorithm for resource allocation from the BS to UE and evaluate user access throughput.

In MIMO systems, multiple refers to the streams that the source sends by multiple transmit antennas. These streams go through a matrix channel, which is composed of all N_t, N_r paths between the N_t and N_r. N_t stands for all the antennas at the transmitter and N_r stands for all the antennas at the receiver. Then, the received signal vectors reach to the destination. Likewise, this happens through the multiple receive antennas and it decodes the received signal vectors into the prototype information. A narrowband flat fading MIMO system is modelled by the authors of [11] as:

$$y = Hx + n \quad (3)$$

where y and x are the receive and transmit vectors respectively. H refers to the channel matrix and n represents the noise vector.

In our case UE connects to a Macro Cell BS for DL asking for a DR that can be provided by a BS, based on DL SINR. In our research, for two UE that are located within the same cell we suppose that there is no interference between them, as they can be equally delegated to non-interfering sets or Resource Block (RB). RB is a flexible resource structure, where the time-frequency spectrum is split into orthogonal RBs [12]. First, *DR* is computed as:

$$DR = B_{RB} * log_2(1 + SINR_{j,i}) \quad (4)$$

where B_{RB} corresponds to the bandwidth of a specific RB and $SINR_{j,i}$ is the signal-to-interference-plus-noise ratio between UE j and BS i. DR is the data rate for the whole system and is equal to the Macro Cell data rate. This helps to achieve higher spectral efficiency. The number of RBs that a UE (suppose UE_j) demands from a particular BS aiming at a desired rate, is computed below:

$$R_{j,i} = \left\lceil \frac{g_i}{B_{RB} * log_2(1 + SINR_{j,i})} \right\rceil \quad (5)$$

where g_j corresponds to the UE throughput demands and DRj refers to the desired Data Rate for the UE_j.

III. Proposed Mechanism

Figure 1 represents the topology of the 5G network we will perform. In order to get a better estimate of the results, our suggested scenario is depicted below.

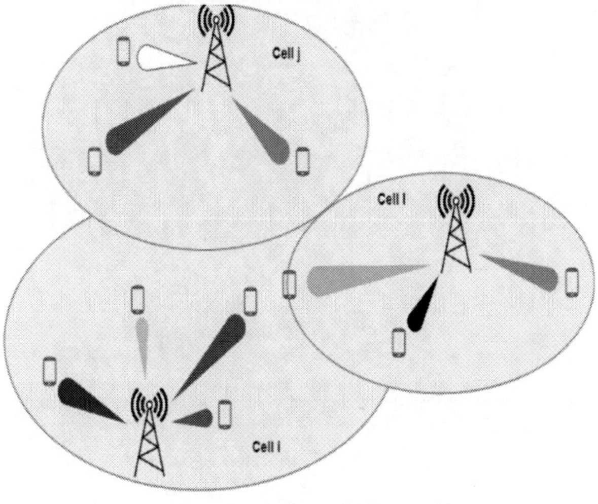

Figure 1. Topology of 5G network.

A. Scenario

We study the case where the maximum number of UE connected to the BS is optimally served. The scenario is depicted in cell i and cell j, where each BS serves more UE at the same time and obtains better beamforming. Later in our simulations we will explain the QoS provided to the UE. This scenario concerns the case of a number of UE who need to be served, whereas some others are located at the limit of a cell, as UE in cell l, who can be served by the BS of either cell i, cell j, or cell l. Obviously, the decision on which BS will serve that UE located at the limits, will be taken using the Knapsack Algorithm approach. In this way, we try to improve existing solutions from previous research that use the KP formulation, aiming at achieving a high level of QoS for all UE.

B. Knapsack Problem (KP)

For the purpose of reaching a satisfying level of QoS, in our approach we apply the 0-1 Knapsack Algorithm. The KP is an implementation of combinatorial optimization. Considering a set of objects, each with weight (w_i) and value (v_i), it determines the number of each object in a collection so that the total weight is less than or equal to a given threshold (W) and the total value is as high as possible. Given a set of items (suppose n items) we want to maximize our profit [13]:

$$\sum_{i=1}^{n} U_i X_i \quad (6)$$

We assume that we have a bag that can hold a set of m ($m < n$) item. For each item we define a variable X_i. With this said, we set $X_i = 1$, when an item belongs in the set of selected items, or $X_i = 0$, when an item is not chosen. Apparently, according to the previous equation (6), for our set of selected items:

$$\sum_{i=1}^{n} U_i X_i \leq W \quad (7)$$

U_i represents the value of the item in the knapsack and W represents the knapsack's capacity. Thus, the goal is to maximize the sum of the values of the items, so that the sum of the weights, is less than or equal to the knapsack's limited space (W). We study the case of a resource allocation technique using the KP algorithm, from the BS to the available antennas. The main goal is to evaluate user access throughput to the antennas. Every BS has the same threshold (W) and is ready to serve the UE. Three variables are considered. The number of BS in our topology scheme, the number of UE and a counter for the total weight. As the BSs are allocated with equal RB (W) and while the counter for the total weight is lower or equal to the given threshold (W), we check the weight and value for each UE. There are two actions that take place. First of all we have to check that UE's weight (w_i) is less than the given threshold and if so, we add the value of this UE (v_i) to a list. Obviously, if UE's weight (w_i) is greater than the given threshold, we reject that UE right away and continue to the next UE. Next, each BS checks the list and allocates RB to all the UE that have the smallest v_i, until the counter is less or equal than W.

More specifically, for our KP, w_i is considered as the bandwidth that the UE needs and v_i, as the distance of the UE from the BS. Moreover, in our KP we define (X_i) and $X_i = 1$, when a UE belongs in the list or $X_i = 0$, when a UE is not selected. Therefore, our mechanism is trying to serve the biggest number of UE with the minimum distance from the BS, in an optimal performance. Although the results presented depict calculations, in which a smaller number of users was used at every base station, the resource allocation mechanism is proposed in a Ma-MIMO system.

Algorithm 1 Resource Allocation Mechanism for UE – A KP Formulation

```
Number of BS_j
Number of UE_i
for each BS_j do
  allocate same RB (W)
    for each UE_i do
      find distance from BS_j
      v_i = distance
      check w_i, v_i
      if w_i < W then
        create list with w_i, v_i
      end if
      else reject UE_i and check next
        while counter <= W do
          check list and allocate RB to UE_i with the
          minimum v_i
        end while
    end for
end for
```

Figure 2. Proposed Algorithm

Considering the proposed mechanism and based on the System Model that was presented above, in the next Section we will describe each parameter needed for the results.

IV. Simulation Setup

In this Section, each parameter needed for the simulations that will be executed in MATLAB is described, while the simulations are given in the next Section.

The air interface defined by the 3rd Generation Partnership Project (3GPP) for 5G is known as New Radio (NR). Frequency bands for 5G NR are divided into two different frequency ranges. Frequency Range 1 (FR1) below 6 GHz and Frequency Range 2 (FR2), each with different capabilities. According to the authors of [14], the range of channel bandwidth defined for FR2 is 50 MHz up to 400 MHz, with two-channel aggregation supported in 3GPP Release 15. Frequencies of up to 300 GHz are used in 5G systems. The higher the frequency, the greater the ability to support high data transfer speeds without interfering with other wireless signals or becoming very cluttered. We will now describe in Table I all the parameters needed for our mechanism.

TABLE I. Default Parameters

Parameter	Setting
COST Hata Model	Macro Cells
Network Deployment	19 Macro Cells
Transmission	MIMO
UE Distribution	Uniform Distribution
Number of UE (K)	100/200/500/1000
DL Bandwidth in BS	400 MHz
UL Bandwidth in UE	(50-400 MHz) – randomly generated

In our simulations we consider an area that consists of 19 Macro Cells (omni directional with an inter-site distance of 375m), as shown below in Figure 3. Macro Cells are used in suburban, city and rural areas. Regarding the simulation deployment scenario, our simulation network contains a different number of UE (*K*). We will model its performance for K UE. First, we consider a BS that has a total Bandwidth of 400MHz (*W*) and there are 100 UE that need to be served. Then, we consider a BS that has a total Bandwidth of 400MHz (*W*) and there are 200 UE that need to be served. We also consider a BS that again has a total Bandwidth of 400MHz (*W*) and there are 500 UE that need to be served. Finally, we consider a BS that has a total Bandwidth of 400MHz (*W*) and there are 1000 UE that need to be served. In each example, the distance of the UE from the BS is estimated (v_i), whereas in each example the demands for bandwidth from each UE differ (w_i) and are randomly generated.

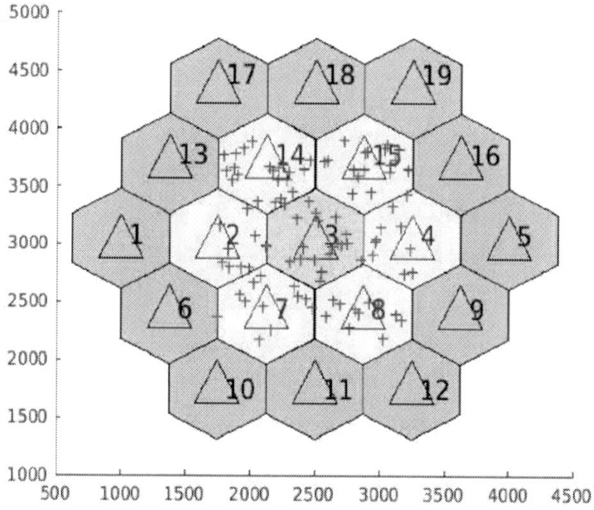

Figure 3. MATLAB simulated network.

Macro cells are depicted in Figure 3 as black triangles, whereas UE are depicted as red crosses.

V. Simulation Results

In this Section, we analyze our experiments for multi-cell systems with random UE positions. In the simulations executed in MATLAB, we used every parameter described above and the results are given below. The figures given below are from our simulations with 100 UE, while the DL Bandwidth in each BS is 400 MHz and the DL Bandwidth in each UE, is randomly generated in the interval [50-400 MHz]. Note that our Network Deployment is 19 Macro Cells but in Figure 3, UE are distributed in 7 Macro Cells. Nevertheless, the proposed mechanism is applied to our COST Hata Model, which includes 19 Macro Cells. These values were chosen for our parameters, in order to present the experiments in a better way.

To start with, the simulated network is described. We consider 100 UE that demand resources of our network. All UE are randomly generated with a personalized chance of appearing inside our area of interest that is served from a Macro Cell. Moreover, in the UpLink (UL) network, all UE have their personalized demands for Bandwidth that ranges from 50 – 400 MHz. As for the DL network, the Bandwidth is equal at all BS at 400MHz.

Concerning the simulation of our experiments, our simulated network with 100 UE, is depicted in Figure 3. Each UE's position is random and we simulated our experiments for a different number of UE. In this way, we create the value of distance between each UE and all the BSs. The signal power that the BS sends is proportional to the reciprocal distance between each UE and the BS. That is the reason why all active UE receive a signal power with the same intensity. The authors of [15] refer to this method as power control, supposing that the signal power that the BS sends changes continually, proportionally to the requirement. Following the above information, in Figure 4, the number of UE that normally connects to each BS, is presented with different colors, according to the minimum distance between them.

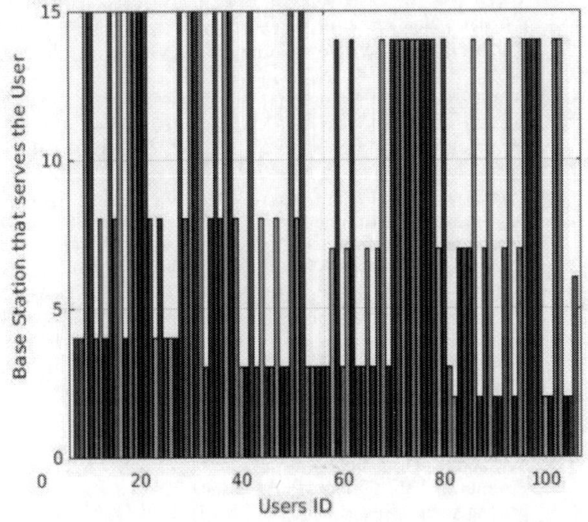

Figure 4. Number of UEs connected to the BS according to minimum distance.

Foremost, if the BS is transmitting data to the UE with a target SNR, the transmitted signal designed is based on the distance between the BS and the UE. To be more specific, if the distance between the Macro Cell and the UE is small, then the Macro Cell is capable of satisfying the target SNR. What is more, it performs that with a small transmit power. In other words, the signal that the Macro Cell sends includes some details about the distance between the Macro Cell and the UE [16]. In Figure 4, we can clearly see what the topology scheme shows us in Figure 3. More particularly, Figure 4 shows us exactly in which Macro Cell each UE will connect, under normal conditions. That means each UE's distance from each BS is computed and therefore we know which BS will serve the UE, according to the minimum distance between them.

Furthermore, in our experiments we continued applying the KP formulation to our mechanism and the three parameters needed were defined. Considering a number of UE as our set of objects, each of them has its demands for bandwidth, which is shown below as each UE's weight. The minimum distance for each UE was also defined, which determines the value. Finally, the total Bandwidth in each BS is 400 MHz and constitutes the given threshold. Our goal is to find the best Knapsack. Given a set of UE we want to maximize our profit, which in our case means that the best total value is a sum of all the values that are included in the KP. Hence, this can be considered as a small modification to the KP, because in this occasion, the value parameter is defined as the minimum distance between each UE and the BS. The bandwidth of each UE (w_i) and the total Bandwidth of every BS (W), are shown below in Figure 5.

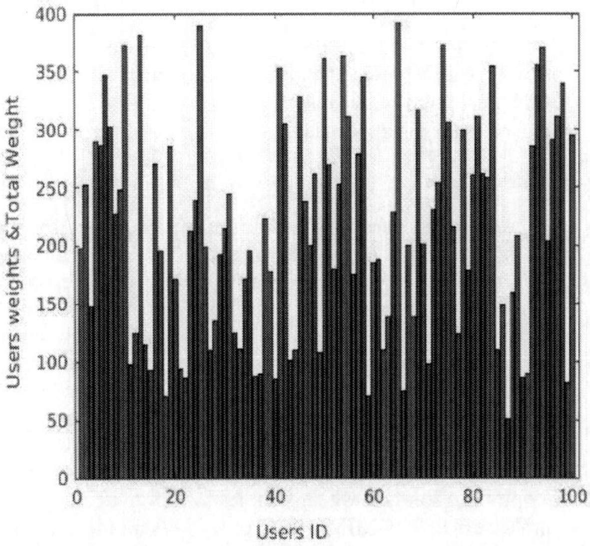

Figure 5. Number of each UE's weight connected to BS with total weight of 400MHz.

Finally, after our KP formulation and the resource allocation, Figure 6 presents the values of the best possible Knapsack in each BS. The value of the best possible Knapsack is computed as the sum of all the minimum distances of the UE that can be served by the BS, based on their weights that is each UE's quantity for bandwidth that they demand. Moreover, in every Knapsack formulation, the "amount of use" of each UE that is served by the BS was also computed. This refers to the variable X_i, which is $X_i = 1$, when a UE is selected to be served by the BS and $X_i = 0$, when a UE is not selected. This amount was computed for every UE in every BS. The "amount of use" of each UE, represents which UE were served by every BS. Therefore, the best possible Knapsack in each BS, is trying to serve the biggest number of UE with the minimum distance from each BS, in an optimal performance, as shown below in Figure 6.

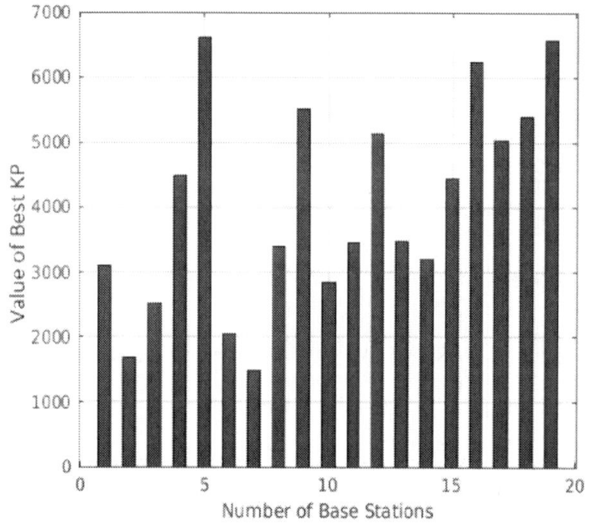

Figure 6. Number of BS and the value of best Knapsack for each BS.

From the above simulations we can clearly see that the results are different in each BS, but comparatively the values of the best possible Knapsack are optimal, as the distance in most of them remains small.

VI. Conclusion And Future Work

From the produced results, the conclusion made, is that the KP formulation is a good technique to use when there is a great need to serve a maximum number of UE, with an optimum QoS, in respect of the achieved Bandwidth. Further research should be done using the KP formulation in a network deployment with Macro Cells and Pico Cells, where Macro Cells serve UE with the maximum distance, while Pico Cells serve UE with the minimum distance. In this way, the QoS in each UE will definitely be improved. More research is needed in Ma-MIMO when using KP formulation, as it can be an optimum solution when it comes to serving the maximum number of UE. Ma-MIMO technology uses multiple antennas at the transmitter and the receiver and this can be a great advantage for further research using KP formulation, in a sense of separating the UE in clusters, while each cluster will be served by the appropriate type of cell. Thus, each UE can be served optimally in a KP formulation, as each BS will serve the respective percentage of UE concerning their minimum distance. Again, this will offer each UE a great QoS, while it can reduce interference.

Finally, the rapid increasing of the data volume in mobile networks forces researchers to study Deep Learning. Machine Learning used in Ma-MIMO can produce different scenarios when using KP formulation, while it can supply us the tools to modify these mechanisms in real time and predict UE's and BS's behavior.

References

[1] A. Gupta and R. K. Jha, "A Survey of 5G Network: Architecture and Emerging Technologies," in IEEE Access, vol. 3, pp. 1206-1232, 2015.

[2] N. Ferdosian, M. Othman, B. Mohd Ali, and K. Yeah Lun, "Greedy–knapsack algorithm for optimal downlink resource allocation in LTE networks", Springer Science+Business Media New York, vol. 22, no. 22, pp. 1427–1440, 2016.

[3] R. Husbands, Q. Ahmed, and J. Wang, "Transmit antenna selection for massive MIMO: A knapsack problem formulation," 2017 IEEE International Conference on Communications (ICC), Paris, 2017, pp. 1-6.

[4] J. Jing and X. Zheng, "A Downlink Max-SINR Precoding for Massive MIMO System", International Journal of Future Generation and Networking, vol. 7, no. 3, pp. 107-116, 2014.

[5] K. Ishimiya, J. Langbacka, Z. Ying, and J. Takada, "A Compact MIMO DRA Antenna," 2008 International Workshop on Antenna Technology: Small Antennas and Novel Metamaterials, Chiba, 2008, pp. 286-289.

[6] E. G. Larsson, O. Edfors, F. Tufvesson, and T. L. Marzetta, "Massive MIMO for next generation wireless systems," in IEEE Communications Magazine, vol. 52, no. 2, pp. 186-195, 2014.2.

[7] P. D. Selvam and K. S. Vishvaksenan, "Antenna Selection and Power Allocation in Massive MIMO", Radioengineering vol. 27, no. 1, pp. 340-346, 2019.4.

[8] R. S. Blum, "MIMO capacity with interference," in IEEE Journal on Selected Areas in Communications, vol. 21, no. 5, pp. 793-801, 2003.6.

[9] J. Ma, Y. J. Zhang, X. Su, and Y. Yao, "On capacity of wireless ad hoc networks with MIMO MMSE receivers," in IEEE Transactions on Wireless Communications, vol. 7, no. 12, pp. 5493-5503, 2008.12.

[10] B. Wang, Y. Chang, and D. Yang, "On the SINR in Massive MIMO Networks with MMSE Receivers," in IEEE Communications Letters, vol. 18, no. 11, pp. 1979-1982, 2014.11.

[11] M. Nasseri and B. Hamidrezav, "Iterative Channel Estimation Algorithm in Multiple Input Multiple Output Orthogonal Frequency Division Multiplexing Systems", Journal of Computer Science, vol. 6, no. 2, pp. 224–228, 2010.

[12] H. Boostanimehr and V. K. Bhargava, "Unified and Distributed QoS-Driven Cell Association Algorithms in Heterogeneous Networks," in IEEE Transactions on Wireless Communications, vol. 14, no. 3, pp. 1650-1662, 2015.3.

[13] C. Lee, Z. Lee, and S. Su, "A New Approach for Solving 0/1 Knapsack Problem," 2006 IEEE International Conference on Systems, Man and Cybernetics, Taipei, 2006, pp. 3138-3143.

[14] Y. Sano, S. Okuyama, N. Lizasa, T. Takada, K. Ando, and N. Fujimura, "5G Radio Performance and Radio Resource Management Specifications", NTT DOCOMO Technical Journal, vol. 20, no. 3, pp. 79-95, 2019.1.

[15] A. Lebl, D. Mitić, T. Branimir, and Z. Markov, "Determination of Base Station Emission Power Change in a Mobile Network Cell with Movable Users", Radioengineering vol. 27, no. 4, pp. 1174-1182, 2018.9.

[16] L. Zhang, W. Zhou, W. Tang, G. Wu, and Z. Chen, "Estimating the distance between macro base station and users in heterogeneous networks," 2017 14th IEEE Annual Consumer Communications & Networking Conference (CCNC), Las Vegas, NV, 2017, pp. 928-932.

Text to Speech through Bluetooth for People with Special Needs Navigation

Eirini Barri
Department of Computer Engineering and Informatics
University of Patras
Patras, Greece
e-mail: ebarri@ceid.upatras.gr

Christos Bouras
Department of Computer Engineering and Informatics
University of Patras
Patras, Greece
e-mail: bouras@cti.gr

Apostolos Gkamas
University Ecclesiastical Academy of Vella
Ioannina, Greece
e-mail: gkamas@aeavellas.gr

Christina Koulouri
Department of Computer Engineering and Informatics
University of Patras
Patras, Greece
e-mail: christinakoul1995@hotmail.gr

Evangelos Michos
Department of Computer Engineering and Informatics
University of Patras
Patras, Greece
e-mail: emichos@ceid.upatras.gr

Spyridon Aniceto Katsampiris Salgado
Department of Computer Engineering and Informatics
University of Patras
Patras, Greece
e-mail: ksalgado@ceid.upatras.gr

***Abstract*—As far as outdoor navigation is considered, the Global Positioning System (GPS) technology is still one of the most (if not the most) commonly used approaches. Even though it is still considered an ideal solution for navigating in outdoor areas, challenges and problems arise when GPS is considered for navigation inside buildings due to the fact that GPS signals cannot penetrate walls/ceilings (e.g., shopping malls, hospitals, etc.) and because signals can be absorbed by the building walls. This paper's contribution is navigation system that assists people with special needs with an audio guidance system that incorporates input from a voice recognition system. The central part of the system is a device that is able to identify the position and orientation of the person that carries it and provides the ability to navigate and route by voice commands. The suggested voice synthesis system is used, so as to guide the user through obstacles in indoor locations. The information of the precise location and orientation of the device is made available to the whole system, through the building's network infrastructure, so that the user's mobile phone, being connected to the same network and also to the user's headset through BLE, is able to send audio commands. For the voice commands, Google Cloud Text-To-Speech (TTS) will be used, assuming that an online connection is active on the user's device.**

Keywords-GuideMe; GPS; BLE; TTS; indoor; navigation; trilateration; pathfinding; audio; voice.

I. INTRODUCTION

Undoubtedly, there is an increasing demand for efficient indoor navigation systems, demand that mainly derives from smart cities, robots and visually impaired people, only to name a few. As far as outdoor navigation and pathfinding are concerned, the Global Positioning System (GPS) is still considered among the most commonly used technologies. Yet, this is only efficiently applicable in outdoor locations, because when indoor navigation comes into play, issues do rise. Of course, indoor navigation is very important to us and has many applications for humans and robots. Two of the most common issues that arise are a) when facing physical obstacles inside buildings that cannot be labeled as obstacles by the GPS and b) the fact that signals cannot be absorbed by walls inside buildings. Multiple floors, rooms and obstacles inside each and every indoor area we can think of pose a major problem. Additionally, the inability to use the GPS technology inside buildings makes indoor navigation more complicated, for reasons already explained above [1].

Many recent studies have been and are still conducted in order to make indoor navigation more effective and efficient. The direct need for new applications and technologies that can efficiently tackle such issues can luckily be covered by other available indoor navigation technologies that do exist nowadays, such as Wireless-Fidelity (Wi-Fi), Bluetooth and sensors.

Some of the most promising technologies for indoor positioning are Bluetooth Low-Energy (BLE) beacons [2] and Ultra-Wide Band (UWB) beacons [3]. More specifically, such beacons have a low deployment cost and are suitable for a wide range of mobile devices. BLE and UWB beacons have undoubtedly great potential because:

- After installation of such beacons, the only equipment needed is a smartphone that incorporates BLE support, whereas foot-mounted positioning needs special inertial sensors.
- The BLE approach supports a large variety of mobile devices (both Android and IOS devices).

- The installation cost of UWB and BLE beacons is relatively low. After deployment, beacons continue to operate for a long duration using their batteries, due to the very low energy consumption rates.

This paper provides the design and development of a navigation system that assists people with special needs using an audio guidance system that incorporates input from a voice recognition system. At its core, the system consists of a device that provides the ability to navigate and route by voice commands, based on the device's location and orientation capabilities. The instructions are based on the device's location and orientation capabilities and this device shall be connected to the server via the user's mobile phone (Android). The suggested voice synthesis system is used to guide the user through obstacles in indoor locations. Wireless connection between the user's mobile phone and the mobile device are made available through low energy consumption BLE and UWB protocols. The overall system (when completed) will consist of the following components:

- Equipment permanently installed in selected areas.
- A cloud server that will synchronize and coordinate the various parts, store information about the facilities and users, and will be responsible for the accounting and invoicing parts.
- Portable devices.
- Software that will run on smartphones.

As far as the voice commands are concerned, Google Cloud Text-To-Speech (TTS) will be used that supports different programming languages through its Application Programming Interface (API) (C#, GO, JAVA, NODE.JS, HYPERTEXT PREPROCESSOR (PHP), PYTHON, RUBY) [4]. The API uses online resources (thus, an active network connection is mandatory) and is provided as a service, or free, or comes with a small cost. The commands for the TTS conversion are provided through Speech Synthesis Markup Language (SSML) language [5]. The GuideMe device will give commands through UWB beacons to the Android application of GuideMe and the application – using the Google Cloud TTS - shall provide the audio commands.

The rest of this paper is organized as follows. Section II describes the motivation behind our work. Section III provides a literature review of other current works on this subject. Section IV addresses the system's architecture whereas Section V goes into finer details in regard to the proposed algorithm for TTS through Bluetooth navigation in indoor spaces. Finally, Section VI summarizes our main findings and conclusions and suggests probable future work. The acknowledgement and conclusions close the article.

II. Motivation

Blindness is the condition of lacking visual perception due to physiological or neurological factors. People with blindness encounter many problems in everyday life. Blind people always depend on others. They can not move easily from one place to another without help from others.

According to World Health Association [31] the following are the key facts regarding blindness and vision impairment

- Globally, at least 2.2 billion people have a vision impairment or blindness, of whom at least 1 billion have a vision impairment that could have been prevented or has yet to be addressed.
- This 1 billion people includes those with moderate or severe distance vision impairment or blindness due to unaddressed refractive error, as well as near vision impairment caused by unaddressed presbyopia.
- Globally, the leading causes of vision impairment are uncorrected refractive errors and cataracts.
- The majority of people with vision impairment are over the age of 50 years.

The GuideMe project [30] will develop a platform that provides guidance and security for out-of-home travel. The solution is built around a discreet portable device capable of indoors localization with accuracy of 10 cm using UWB technology. The device can also determine the orientation of the user, receive voice commands, and transmit voice instructions. It is also capable of detecting crashes and sending updates. The feature is based on the collaboration of a mobile device, a service running on the user's mobile phone and a server.

The motivation of the paper is to improve two areas in the life of the blind people and people with special needs in general: convenience and security. Specifically, with the use of the proposed system, users will feel more comfortable visiting public places such as airports, shopping malls, stations, etc., as they will be guided by the system to reach their destination. At the same time, in case of emergencies involving both the user (accidents) and the building (fire, earthquake etc.), the system will inform the users of the exact location of the users, whilst also guiding them to the nearest exit. The ultimate goal is to increase the presence of the population with mobility or other problems in buildings by 20%.

III. Related Work

In this section, we present previous research work on indoor navigation systems targeted for people with special needs and provide a summarized overview of the research conducted in this field. Our literature review is categorized in research work on indoor positioning and indoor navigation.

Following the previous studies, in this section, we will present similar projects to GuideMe. Indoo.rs and San Francisco International Airport worked together to create an app for visually impaired passengers. The Entrepreneurship-in-Residence (EIR) project is an Edwin M. Lee collaboration with the White House and other San Francisco business partners. At the beginning of 2014, they chose to help the San Francisco Airport (SFO) create a tool to assist blind and visually impaired travelers [11].

Recommendation ITU-T F.921 [12] determines the way a navigation system that is audio-based can be developed to guarantee that it is dedicated and responsive to the needs of people with visual disabilities. It takes on a technologically neutral approach and sets the operating attributes of the system. The goal is to provide visual network system designers with the audio data they require in the early stages of development to prevent any problems that keep vision impaired users from making full and independent use of the built environment. This system explains how to adapt the user experience to audio-based network navigation systems and to secure the interoperability of these technologies. In addition, it acknowledges that, to meet the needs of people that are visually impaired, networked audio navigation systems can also benefit people with other age-related disabilities, as well as the general public.

The purpose of [13] is to implement a module-based application developed in the context of preliminary projects for the mobile mass market, through an appropriate user interface that responds to the needs of the visually impaired. The blind user should be able to use public transport independently in a secure manner and navigate complex public transport terminals. As a result, the system combines real-time communication to and from public transport vehicles with precise positioning and guidance while it also provides additional navigation assistance.

Same as [13], INK 2016, Indoor Navigation and Communication in ÖPNV for blind and visually impaired people [14], combines real-time communication to and from public transport vehicles with precise positioning and guidance and has additional video call navigation assistance where the person can communicate with a professional operator.

Project Ways4all [15] is a new personalized indoor navigation system that can increase public transport accessibility for all passengers and especially the visually impaired, who will be able to access public transport and the necessary up-to-date traffic information in a very simplified way.

Finally, project "Using an Integrated Technique for Developing Indoor Navigation Systems to Allow the Blind and Visually Impaired People to Reach Precise Objects" [16], uses a set of different technologies (WiFi, Bluetooth, and Radio-frequency Identification (RFID)) to help the user reach a micro element in the navigated environment. As a proof of concept, Yarmouk University will test the system framework on their library to help the blind user find a specific book. Therefore, it constitutes an intelligent interface for precise indoor navigation for blind and visually impaired people using a smart phone.

A. Text-To-Speech (TTS)

In this section, we present previous research work on TTS techniques targeted for people with special needs and provide a summarized overview of the research conducted in this field. Our literature review is categorized in research work on TTS and Bluetooth TTS for blind people.

There are several studies concerning TTS. Speech synthesis is the artificial production of human speech. Attempts to control the quality of voice of synthesized speech, several prototypes and fully operating systems have been built based on different synthesis techniques. The authors of [17] review recent advances in research and development of speech synthesis, so as to provide a technological perspective. Their approach is based on the Hidden Markov Model (HMM) and aims to summarize and compare the characteristics of various speech synthesis techniques used by presenting their advantages and disadvantages.

The purpose of [18] is to try to explain the aim of a TTS synthesis system and how it works. In more detail, the authors try to give a short and inclusive review of developing a system that is equal to human performance. The rule-based techniques (formant and articulatory synthesis) are described by the authors and, finally, they propose an HMM synthesis combined with a Harmonic plus Noise Model (HNM), so as to get a TTS synthesis system that requires lower development time and cost.

As mentioned before, the commands for the TTS conversion are provided through SSML language [5]. SSML is a component of a bigger set of markup specifications for voice browsers developed through the open processes of the W3C. It is scheduled to provide a rich, XML-based markup language in order to assist the generation of synthetic speech in Web and other applications. A TTS system (a synthesis processor) that supports SSML will be responsible for providing a document as spoken output. It will also be responsible for using the details contained in the markup to provide the document, as intended by the author. According to [18], a significant job of the markup language is to provide authors of synthesizable content a standard way to control some characteristics of speech such as pronunciation, volume, pitch, rate, etc. across different synthesis-capable platforms.

Special reference needs to be made on the API for TTS services. The GuideMe device will give commands through UWB beacons to the Android application of GuideMe and the application – using the Google Cloud TTS -shall provide the audio commands. Particularly, [20] refers to a Cloud TTS conversion powered by machine learning. Google Cloud TTS transmutes text into human-like speech. This is accomplished in more than 180 voices across 30 variants and languages, or more. It applies groundbreaking research in speech synthesis (WaveNet) and Google's powerful neural networks to deliver high-fidelity audio. With this easy-to-use API, anyone can make live interactions with users that constitute customer service, device interaction, and other applications.

Another API for TTS service is [21]. This is part of the Speech service of Microsoft and builds apps and services that speak naturally. This API creates lifelike voices with the Neural Text to Speech capability built on breakthrough research in speech synthesis technology. It offers a wide range of voices and languages. One specific characteristic of this API is that it provides its users with models for customization in order to create a unique voice for everyone's solution and brand.

Similar to [21], another part of the Speech service of Microsoft is [22]. Respectively, it allows to convert text into synthesized speech and get a list of supported voices for a region using a set of REST APIs. Each available endpoint is associated with a region. Also, a subscription key for the endpoint / region someone plans to use is required. The differentiation from [21] is that TTS REST API supports neural and standard TTS voices, each of which supports a specific language and dialect, identified by locale.

Watson is IBM's suite of enterprise-ready AI services, applications, and tooling. Watson TTS [23] converts written text into natural-sounding audio in a variety of languages and voices. Watson TTS develops interactive toys for children, automates call center interactions, communicates directions hands-free, and beyond. It delivers a seamless voice interaction that caters to the audience with control over every word. Like [21], it offers this pronunciation across many languages and voices, which is very important for the users.

It is important to mention that every API for TTS service described above includes documentation, in order to facilitate usage and implementation by the users.

B. *Bluetooth TTS for blind people*

In [24], the PERCEPT system is introduced. PERCEPT is an indoor navigation system for the people who have visual issues and cannot see. PERCEPT is intended to make improvements to the quality of life and health of the visually impaired community and try to give the ability for independent living. Using PERCEPT, blind users are supposed to access public health facilities such as clinics, hospitals, and wellness centers, without the help of other people, but only using their own means. PERCEPT system tests were held with the participation of 24 blind and visually impaired users in a multilevel building. The results show that PERCEPT system is effective in providing the right navigation instructions to these users. The key aspects and advantages of this system are that it is inexpensive and that its design follows orientation and mobility principles, according to the authors.

The creators of the PERCEPT system have also created the INSIGHT system [25], which is an indoor location tracking and navigation system for the blind people using RFID (Radio Frequency Identification) and Bluetooth connectivity technologies. The workflow is as follows. The PDA based user device interacts with the INSIGHT server and provides the user navigation instructions through voice commands. They have implemented accurate navigation as well they have integrated a PANIC button in case of emergency. Moreover, the system is able to understand if the user is in wrong place and heads towards false direction and helps them to re-route in order to move in the correct direction.

In [26], a system with a portable TTS converter is designed in order to assist the blind listen to an audio of a text that has been scanned. The system, according to the authors, consists of a page scanner that can be carried with one hand, an Android phone that is able to scan the image and send it over Bluetooth, and an app that helps with the extraction of the text from the scanned image and to convert the extracted text to speech. Moreover, another positive impact of this system is that it comes with a page scanner which scans the entire page containing the text. So, blind users do not need to take photos and focus on the area of text that is needed, and then crop it in order to remove the background pictures etc, something that happens in the case of other systems that exist.

Furthermore, [27] tries to design and create a solution for visually impaired travelers and specifically, for the use case of train transportation using only a smartphone and no other hardware. Particularly, using the BLE and the integrated compass of the smartphone, the system is able to provide turn by turn voice commands inside the Tokyo station.

In [28], the authors designed a system for visually impaired people in order to help them navigate through work zones in a safer manner. According to statistics taken from the Federal Highway Administration (FHWA), every year about 17% of all work zone fatal accidents happen to pedestrians [28]. People who have problems seeing often must deal with physical and information difficulties that limit their accessibility and mobility. After a survey conducted, some elements of the results were implemented in a smartphone application that incorporates both GPS and Bluetooth technologies to calculate the user's location. When the user goes to a work zone, the smartphone is supposed to vibrate, so as to alert users, and the application will then announce an appropriate audible message to users. Blind users, if they want, they could do a single tap on the smartphone to repeat the audio messages.

IV. System Architecture

In this project, the main components are a small wearable that helps in the user's positioning through Ultra-Wide Band (UWB) technology. This technology provides very accurate positioning, up to 10 cm divergence. The system, apart from the ability to locate the user, has the ability to provide guidance via voice commands.

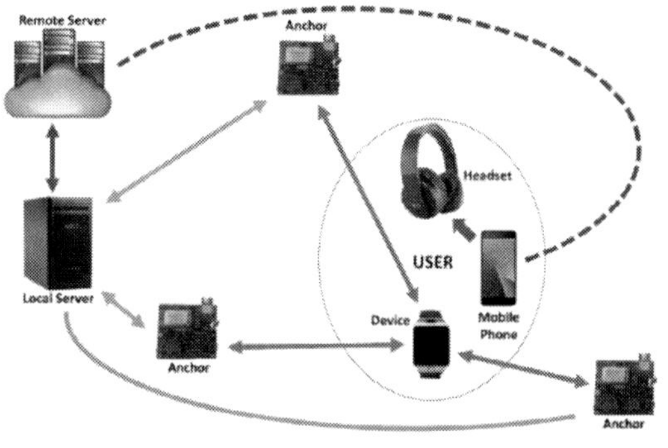

Figure 1. Overview of the proposed architecture.

In our purposed system, our smart device can communicate to anchors via UWB technology, in order to locate the user. The anchors are calculating and measuring the distance between the user and the anchor. The distance data (between the user and the anchors) is transferred to a local server so as to measure the exact position, running positioning algorithms. The local server, based on the positioning and navigation algorithms, will give commands (using the Wi-Fi network) to the Android application of GuideMe running on the user's Android smart phone and the application – using the Google Cloud TTS - shall provide the audio commands. The API uses online resources and is provided as a service. The commands for the TTS conversion are provided through SSML language. Furthermore, there is a remote server that has a map of the building. This remote server, having the details of the building, the position of the user and the destination of the user, can provide guidance to the user, giving him directions. The directions are given by the smartphone to the user through wireless headphones, using voice commands. The system will also support the usage of pre-recorded voice command for the case where no Internet access is available.

As far as the wearable device is concerned, the processor that is chosen is the module made by Esspresif (Esspresif ESP32 [33]). This family of processors are energy efficient, in order to expand the battery life. A Wi Fi module is integrated as well in the system. For the connectivity through UWB, we have chosen the module DWM1000 of Decawave [32].

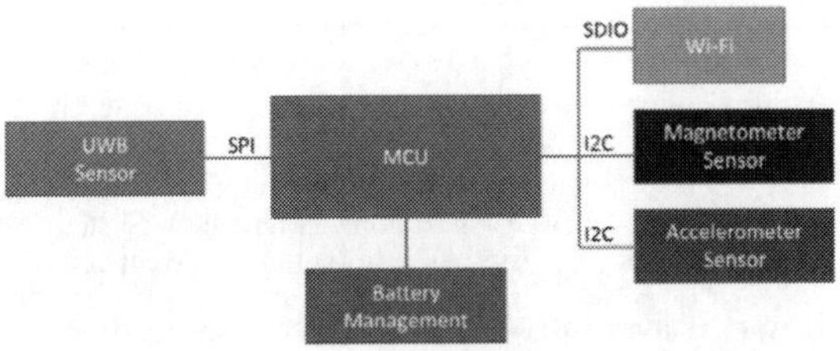

Figure 2. Overview of the device's architecture

Figure 2 presents the general architecture of the device. The device consists of the magnetometer and accelerometer sensors, the UWB module, the Main Computing Unit and a module for the battery management as well.

V. PROPOSED SYSTEM

In this section, we describe the proposed system for TTS through Bluetooth navigation in indoor spaces. We propose a GuideMe device that will use UWB beacons to let the system identify its position and orientation precisely and provide this information to the Android application of GuideMe and the application – using the Google Cloud TTS- shall provide the audio commands. The commands for the TTS conversion are provided through SSML language. SSML is a component of a bigger set of markup specifications for voice browsers developed through the open processes of the W3C. It is scheduled to provide a rich, XML-based markup language in order to assist the generation of synthetic speech in Web and other applications. A TTS system (a synthesis processor) that supports SSML will be responsible for providing a document as spoken output. It will also be responsible for using the details contained in the markup to provide the document, as intended by the author. According to [18], a significant job of the markup language is to provide authors of synthesizable content a standard way to control some characteristics of speech such as pronunciation, volume, pitch, rate, etc. across different synthesis-capable platforms.

Special reference needs to be made on the API for TTS services. TTS is considered ideal for any application that plays an audio of human speech to users [29]. TTS operates by converting SSML input into audio data and by using TTS. The response string can be converted to actual human speech that will be played back to the user of the application. As for the process, the procedure of translating text input into audio data is called synthesis and the output is labeled as synthetic speech. The speech synthesis begins by generating raw audio data as a base64-encoded string and decoding of this string into an audio file is required in order to play from the application. Additionally, TTS offers a large variety of custom voices, depending on the needs (voices differ by language, gender and accent). The output settings are also configurable, concerning speaking rate, pitch, volume and sample rate hertz.

An indicative mode of the operation, followed by the system we described, is shown in Figure 3.

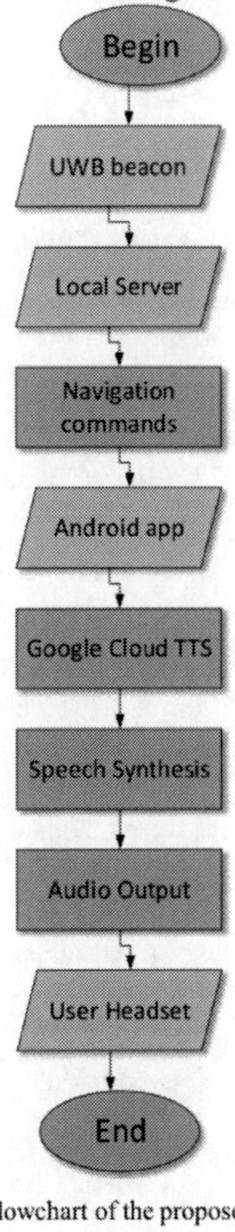

Figure 3. Flowchart of the proposed system

VI. CONCLUSION AND FUTURE WORK

This work refers to the project GuideMe using Bluetooth technology for text-to-speech directions given to people with visual difficulties. Some previous research works on indoor navigation systems using text-to-speech technology were presented. This work is the basis of the next step of the project that relates to developing the software for smartphone or a wearable device using an audio guidance system that incorporates input from a voice recognition system. The text-to-speech technology through Bluetooth is used to guide the user through obstacles in indoor locations. For future work, we may include an extension of this current research by also covering outdoor areas through the application.

ACKNOWLEDGMENT

This research has been co-financed by the European Union and Greek national funds through the Regional Operation Program "Western Greece 2014-2020", under the Call "Regional research and innovation strategies for smart specialization (RIS3) in Communication and Information Technologies" (project code: 5038620 entitled "System for indoors orientation and guidance - GuideMe").

REFERENCES

[1] E. J. Alqahtani, F. H. Alshamrani, H. F. Syed and F. A. Alhaidari, "Survey on Algorithms and Techniques for Indoor Navigation Systems.," in 21st Saudi Computer Society National Computer Conference, Riyadh, pp. 1-9, April, 2018.

[2] Z. Zuo, L. Liu, L. Zhang, and Y. Fang, "Indoor Positioning Based on Bluetooth Low-Energy Beacons Adopting Graph Optimization," Sensors, vol. 18, no. 11, p. 3736, November, 2018.

[3] S. Monica and G. Ferrari, "Impact of the number of beacons in PSO-based auto-localization in UWB networks," In European Conference on the Applications of Evolutionary Computation, Springer, Berlin, Heidelberg, pp. 42-51, April, 2013.

[4] https://cloud.google.com/text-to-speech/docs/ 2020.04.06

[5] https://cloud.google.com/text-to-speech/docs/ssml 2020.04.06

[6] A. bin Mohamed Kassim, T. Yasuno, H. I. Jaafar, and M. A. Mohd Shahrieel, "Development and Evaluation of Voice Recognition Input Technology in Navigation System for Blind Person," Journal of Signal Processing, vol. 19, no. 4, pp. 135–138, 2015.

[7] Natarajan, Thangadurai , Kartheeka, S., "Intelligent Control Systems for Physically Disabled and Elderly People for Indoor Navigation," International Journal for Research in Applied Science and Engineering Technology. vol. 2. pp. 198-205, 2014.

[8] R. K. Megalingam, R. N. Nair and S. M. Prakhya, "Automated voice based home navigation system for the elderly and the physically challenged," in 2nd International Conference on Wireless Communication, Vehicular Technology, Information Theory and Aerospace & Electronic Systems Technology, Chennai, pp. 1-5, 2011.

[9] A. Kishore et al., "CENSE: A Cognitive Navigation System for People with Special Needs," in IEEE Third International Conference on Big Data Computing Service and Applications, San Francisco, CA, pp., 198-203, 2017.

[10] H. A. Karimi, M. B. Dias, J. Pearlman, and G. J. Zimmerman, "Wayfinding and Navigation for People with Disabilities Using Social Navigation Networks," EAI Endorsed Transactions on Collaborative Computing, vol. 1, no. 2, p. e5, Octomber, 2014.

[11] https://indoo.rs/indoo-rs-and-san-francisco-international-airport-unveil-app-for-visually-impaired-passengers/ 2020.04.06

[12] https://www.itu.int/rec/T-REC-F.921-201808-I/en 2020.04.06

[13] https://trimis.ec.europa.eu/project/indoor-navigation-and-communication-public-transport-blind-and-visually-impaired 2020.04.06

[14] https://www.tugraz.at/institute/ifg/projects/navigation/ink/ 2020.04.06

[15] http://www.ways4all.at/index.php/en/ways4all 2020.04.06

[16] http://it.yu.edu.jo/index.php/it-faculty/facutly-projects/123-english-articles/242-using-an-integrated-techniques-for-developing-indoor-navigation-systems-to-allow-the-blind-and-visually-impaired-people-to-reach-precise-objects 2020.04.06

[17] Text-to-Speech Synthesis Techniques Eduardo M. B. de A. Tenorio and Tsang Ing Ren ´Centro de Informatica, Universidade Federal de Pernambuco ´Recife, PE, Brasil – www.cin.ufpe.br 2020.04.06

[18] Helal Uddin Mullah, "Comparative Study of Different Text-to-Speech Synthesis Techniques," International Journal of Scientific , Engineering Research, vol. 6, 287-292, June, 2015

[19] https://www.w3.org/TR/speech-synthesis11/ 2020.04.06

[20] https://cloud.google.com/text-to-speech/ 2020.04.06

[21] https://azure.microsoft.com/en-us/services/cognitive-services/text-to-speech/ 2020.04.06

[22] https://docs.microsoft.com/en-us/azure/cognitive-services/speech-service/rest-text-to-speech 2020.04.06

[23] https://www.ibm.com/watson/services/text-to-speech/ 2020.04.06

[24] A. Ganz, J. Schafer, S. Gandhi, E. Puleo, C. Wilson, and M. Robertson, "PERCEPT Indoor Navigation System for the Blind and Visually Impaired: Architecture and Experimentation," International Journal of Telemedicine and Applications, vol. 2012, pp. 1–12, December, 2012.

[25] A. Ganz, S. R. Gandhi, C. Wilson, and G. Mullett, "INSIGHT: RFID and Bluetooth enabled automated space for the blind and visually impaired," in 2010 Annual International Conference of the IEEE Engineering in Medicine and Biology, 2010.

[26] K. Ragavi, P. Radja, and S. Chithra, "Portable Text to Speech Converter for the Visually Impaired," in Proceedings of the International Conference on Soft Computing Systems, Springer India, pp. 751–758, 2015.

[27] J.-E. Kim, M. Bessho, S. Kobayashi, N. Koshizuka, and K. Sakamura, "Navigating visually impaired travelers in a large train station using smartphone and bluetooth low energy," in Proceedings of the 31st Annual ACM Symposium on Applied Computing - SAC '16, 2016

[28] Development of a Navigation System Using Smartphone and Bluetooth Technologies to Help the Visually Impaired Navigate Work Zones Safely, [Online] file:///C:/Users/owner/AppData/Local/Temp/MnDOT2014-12.pdf 2020.04.06

[29] https://cloud.google.com/text-to-speech/docs/basics 2020.04.06

[30] http://www.guideme-project.upatras.gr 2020.04.06

[31] https://www.who.int/news-room/fact-sheets/detail/blindness-and-visual-impairment 2020.04.06

[32] https://www.decawave.com/product/dwm1000-module/ 2020.04.06

[33] https://www.espressif.com/en/products/hardware/esp32/overview 2020.04.06

Gap in pagination due to unavailable paper.

Pages 19-25

Dynamic Intrusion Deception in a Cloud Environment

Chia-Chi Teng
Cybersecurity
Brigham Young University
Provo, UT, USA
email: ccteng@byu.edu

Aaron Cowley
Cybersecurity
Brigham Young University
Provo, UT, USA
email: acow777@gmail.com

Ressel Havens
Cybersecurity
Brigham Young University
Provo, UT, USA
email: russel.havens@gmail.com

***Abstract*—As cyber-attacks become more sophisticated, Network Intrusion Detection Systems also need to adapt to counter the evolving advanced persistent threats. Security deception, such as Honeypot, is an emerging defense tactic for security operation in enterprise network or commercial cloud environment. A well designed Honeypot can fool attackers and malicious agents into a made-up system that is monitored by security operators who can safely observe the attacks and promptly develop counter measures. However, the availability of Anti-Honeypot technologies has made the deception defense more challenging. A dynamic deception method is necessary to counter the modern Honeypot detection systems. We propose a dynamic intrusion deception method designed to run in a public cloud environment. A prototype of Honeynet is built using the Microsoft Windows Azure Resource Group virtual machines and network management platform.**

Keywords—Cloud Computing; Intrusion Detection; Intrusion Deception; Honeypot; Honeynet.

I. Introduction

Since commercial cloud computing services became available over a decade ago, the cloud computing technology platforms have made significant advancement in research and development. Public cloud providers, such as Microsoft, Amazon, Google and IBM, are offering a large variety of services from infrastructure as a service (IaaS), platform as a service (PaaS) to software as a service (SaaS). Cloud computing is now the backbone of thousands of enterprises and organizations where a 2018 industry study shows 77% of enterprises have at least one application or a portion of their Information Technology (IT) infrastructure in the cloud [1] and trending up. While the industry continues to invest in cloud computing, the study also shows that about one-third of the IT decision-makers saying security concerns is one of their top challenges.

In addition to private enterprises and business, government agencies are also embracing the cloud computing technology to support their future infrastructure and services. For example, United States Department of Defense (DoD) listed cloud computing as one of the top priorities in their Digital Modernization Strategy [2]. DoD has also recently awarded a ten-year ten billion dollar (USD) contract to Microsoft for its Joint Enterprise Defense Infrastructure (JEDI) project [3].

With all the sensitive and classified information being stored in the cloud, the security requirement has also increased. It is important to understand the threat models, attack surfaces, and available controls in the cloud environment to effectively manage the security risks [4].

Intrusion Detection System (IDS) and Intrusion Prevention System (IPS) [5] are well-known security controls commonly deployed in enterprise or cloud computing environment. They can protect target systems based on network or host activities by denying access to malicious attacks. However, IDS/IPS do not usually attempt to discover additional information about the attacks or attackers, which is the primary function of the Honeypot technology.

Honeypots are usually designed to resemble valid systems or services with exploitable vulnerabilities to lure attackers to gain access. When working in conjunction with IDS, attackers' activities are monitored and analyzed by security operators once they are in the Honeypots. Valuable information can be discovered while an attack is taking place.

Unfortunately, Anti-Honeypot technologies have also been developed by spammers and other malicious parties to counter this defense measure. The unique capabilities of public cloud computing platforms can enable a new type of Honeypot that is more dynamic, realistic and cost effective in a way that defensive resources mimicking real targets can be instantiated and configured in real time as malicious attacks are being detected.

A design and prototype of a dynamic Honeypot system is presented below with a review of other recent work on cloud computing related Honeypot and Honeynet. As the system detects potential attacks, such as Brute-force SSH, it dynamically creates containers, re-routes malicious network traffic and actively engages with the attacker to gather information about the attack and attacker. While the preliminary work is implemented and tested on Microsoft Windows Azure platform, it can easily be ported to other public cloud providers.

II. Background

Since the concept of Honeypot was first introduced in 1998 [6], its applications have steadily been gaining popularity and support as Honeypot evolved from a non-traditional tool to one of the commonly used security controls. For example, United States DoD Cloud Computing Security Requirement Guide [7] specifies Honeypot as one of the standard controls. Many varieties of Honeypot intrusion deception systems have been proposed over the years, which can be classified based on their level of interaction, scope, or targeted attack type [8]. A recent survey [9] of Honeypot systems in a cloud environment further classifies them based on architectures and functionalities. These cloud-based solutions include

- Honeynet [10]

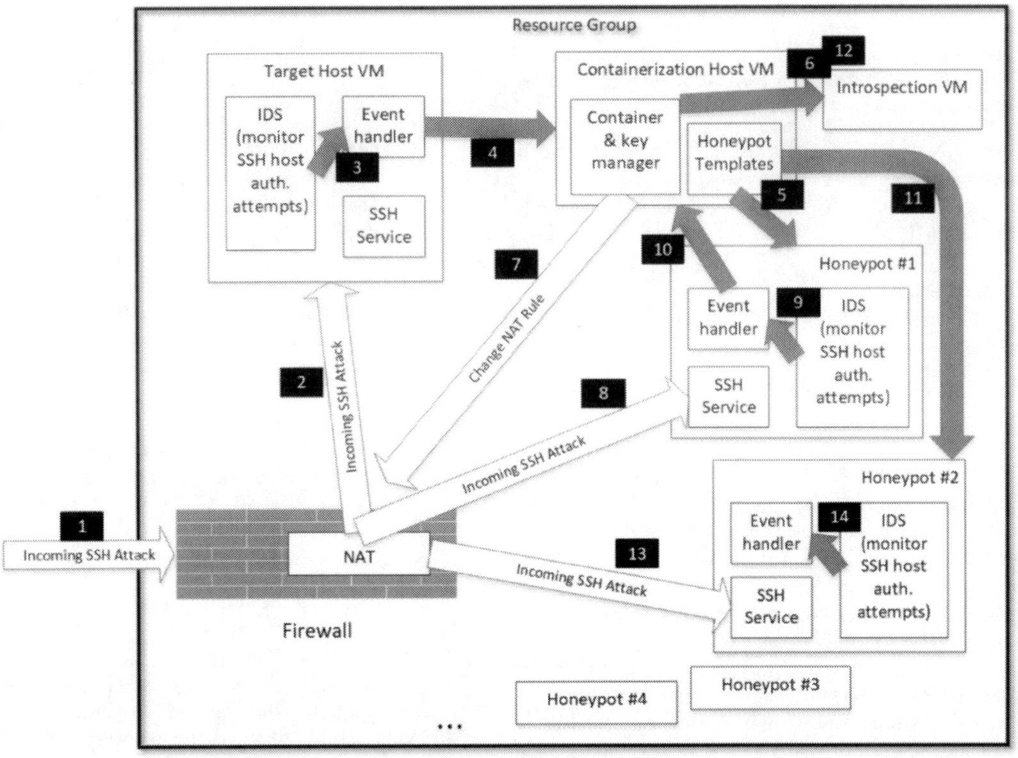

Figure 1. Dynamic Honenet System Diagram

- HoneyFarm [11]
- HoneyBrid [12]
- HoneyMix [13]
- HoneyProxy [14]

Honeypots are usually used as an integrated-component in an defense in depth strategy instead of a standalone security control. Study showed that combining Honeypot with IDS/IPS can increase the success rate of attack detection and prevention [15]. While IDS/IPS can deny access to malicious attack, Honeypot can further gather valuable information, such as attacker's identity and technique [16].

The security community has developed several open-source Honeypot packages where some of them are considered quite mature according to industry evaluation [17]. For example:

- Dionaea [18]: a low-interaction server-side Honeypot that collects network malware.
- Honeyd [19]: a multi-purpose low-interaction Honeypot using virtual hosts and services.
- Kippo [20]: low-interaction SSH Honeypot.
- Glastopf [21]: low-interaction web applications Honeypot.

CloudHoneyCY [22] further proposed an open-source framework to integrate a variety of existing Honeypot, such as the one listed above, to work together in a cloud environment.

SSH is one of the commonly used attack surface against services deployed in the cloud as it is the standard protocol for developers and operators to access the target system. Research shows that Brute-force/dictionary attacks against remote services, such as SSH is ranked among one of the most common forms of attacks that compromise servers [23]. Using Virtual Machine Introspection (VMI) technique with a VM-based SSH Honeypot can be effective in defending against such attacks [24].

Study [25] has shown that new containerization technology, such as Docker [26], can improve Honeypot systems with following advantages over VM-based solutions,

- Scalability: spinning up/down containers is easier.
- Performance: spinning up/down container is faster.
- Cross-platform: containerization is supported by all major cloud providers.
- Cost: contains have smaller CPU and memory footprint which incur lower cost than VM's in typical pay-per-use cloud environments.

The cloud containers will inevitably enable Honeypot or Honeynet to be more dynamic and looks more like a real system. Research and development of container introspection technology has drastically increase the capability of monitoring applications inside containers [27].

Today's cybersecurity is a cat-and-mouse game where threat actors constantly make improvement with their tools to by-pass defensive controls. Anti-honeypot technologies have been successful in identifying and countering low- and medium-interaction Honeypots [28], for example, Honeypot Hunter [29] has been used by spammers to identify HTTP and SOCKS Honeypot proxies. Research [30] showed that a dynamic Honeypot can be effective in defending malicious attacks.

Leveraging the previous research and the latest cloud technology available, we propose a Honeynet system with the following characteristics,

- Dynamically provision and revoke Honeypots based on level of malicious network activities.
- High-interactivity Honeypots with dynamically configured SSH service.
- Use container technology, e.g., Docker, for increased performance and scalability.
- Easily deployable in a commercial cloud platform, e.g., Microsoft Azure.

The design and implementation of the proposed system are discussed below.

III. METHODS

This dynamic Honeynet design is currently targeting commercial public cloud computing services with large user base and mature technology platform. Leading providers, such as Microsoft Azure and Amazon AWS have the concept of "resource group", which is a logical collection of assets grouped together for effective management, such as provisioning, monitoring, and access control. The high-level design of the proposed cloud-based Honeynet system is shown in Figure 1 above in a logical resource group environment. As this system must rely on the cloud provider's resource management interface, e.g., Azure Resource Manager or AWS Resource Access Manager, the actual implementation might be somewhat platform dependent.

A resource group can be setup to include the following collection of items,

- A Firewall and programmable Network Address Translation (NAT) or reverse proxy layer.
- Regular service(s) which might be the initial target(s) of an SSH brute-force attack.
- A target VM containing real services which also monitors network intrusion with an IDS. Event trigger will take place when certain pre-defined malicious activity is observed.
- A VM host for the containerization software run-time, e.g., Docker, which also handles the IDS event triggered by an attack then dynamically provisions and configures Honeypot accordingly.
- Pre-built container template of Honeypot with SSH services and IDS.
- An Introspection VM for monitoring active Honeypots.

In the scenario of a SSH brute-force attack, the following step-by-step actions will take place as labelled in Figure 1.

1) Incoming SSH brute-force attack reaches Firewall and NAT.
2) Attack traffic directed to the target host.
3) After a number of failed SSH login attempts, an IDS event triggers indicating a SSH brute-force attack taking place.
4) The event handler invokes container host services.
5) An initial Honeypot service (#1) container is provisioned, which hosts a simulated SSH service and a pre-configured IDS.
6) Notify the Introspection VM to begin monitoring Honeypot #1.
7) Configure NAT to redirect attacker IP's SSH traffic to the Honeypot service.
8) Incoming SSH attacks now goes to Honeypot #1.
9) IDS detects brute-force SSH attack on Honeypot #1.
10) Invoke container service to create new Honeypot service (#2), generate authorized key for Honeypot #2, then allow attacker to successfully connect to the simulated SSH service where host and authorization information to Honeypot #2 can be found.
11) Honeypot #2 is provisioned.
12) Notify the Introspection VM to begin monitoring Honeypot #2.
13) Attacker attempts connection to Honeypot #2 with the host and authentication information found in Honeypot #1.
14) IDS detects attacker's activity on Honeypot #2 and create new Honeypots as needed.

Depending on the security operator's objective, the steps of detecting malicious activities, provisioning and directing attacker to a new Honeypot can be repeated as needed until certain information about the attacker is discovered, or until the attacker become inactive. The operator can configure the Honeynet based on available resources and desired level of interactivity.

The event handler in the Honeypots can be configured with a timer where it initiates the process of self-revocation or de-provision of the container if certain amount of time elapsed without the attacker actively engaged. The automated Honeypot provision and revocation feature can potentially make the Honeynet more dynamic and better at countering anti-Honeypot technology.

IV. RESULTS

Base on the design described above, a functioning prototype is successfully implemented with the following specifications as shown in Figure 2.

- Cloud computing platform: Microsoft Windows Azure with Azure Virtual Network, Azure Resource Group and Resource Manager.
- Target Host: Ubuntu Linux server running OpenSSH Daemon (sshd).
- IDS: Zeek (formerly Bro) Network Security Monitor.
- Network Address Translation (NAT): Azure Service Fabric Reverse Proxy.
- Container Host: Docker and its Command-Line Interface (CLI), such as "docker run" and "docker cp".

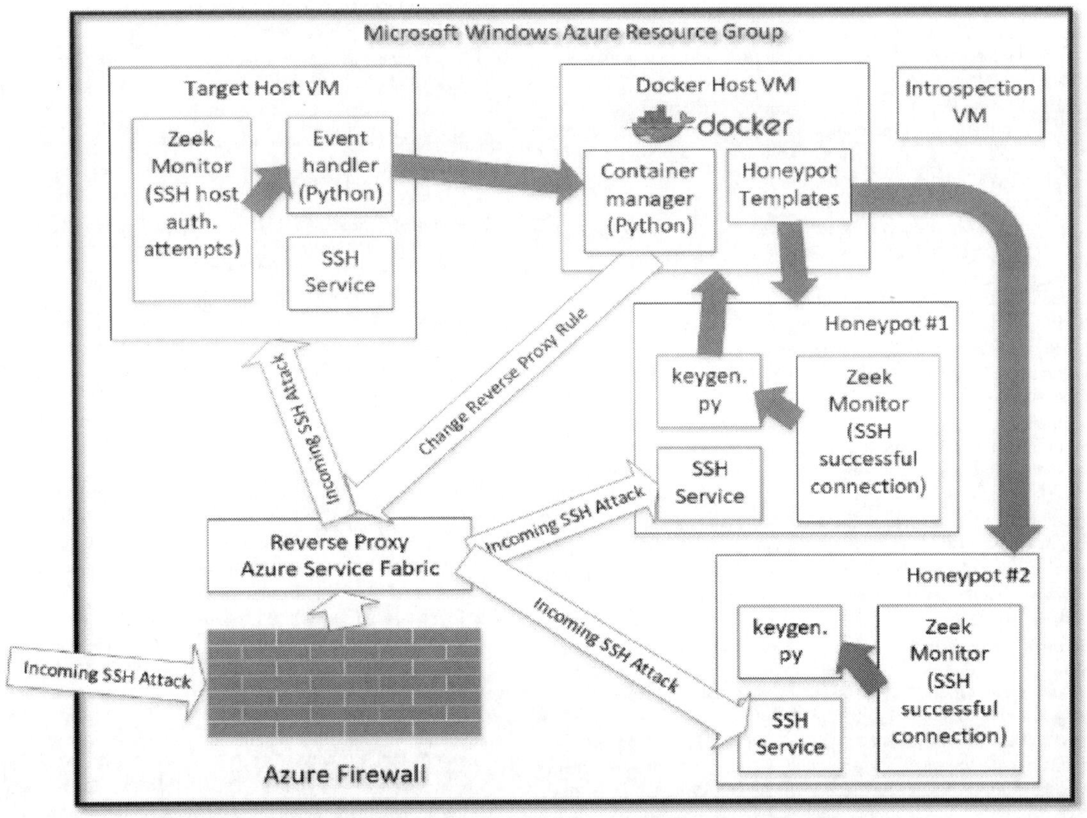

Figure 2. Functional Prototype as Implemented in Microsoft Windows Azure Cloud Environment.

- Two container templates/images: Honeypot #1 is the initial container where the SSH brute force attack is redirected to. Honeypot #2 is the secondary container where the attacker is lured to after allowed successful SSH connection to Honeypot #1.

In the test environment created as an Azure Resource Group, we configured a Zeek trigger to take place after ten failed SSH authentication attempts on the Target Host. The event handler is a Python script that connects to the Docker Host and invoke "docker run" to lunch Honeypot #1. The Python script also collects host information of the attacker and dynamically configure the Azure Reverse Proxy to redirect the SSH attack traffic to Honeypot #1.

If Honeypot #1 continues to see incoming SSH brute force attack, it will invoke another Python script that "docker run" Honeypot #2, then generate a new SSH authorized_keys file and "docker cp" to the newly provision container. At the same time, the Python script will leave bread crumb in Honeypot #1 containing the authorized key to Honeypot #2 for the attacker to find.

The completed Honeynet was blind tested by multiple penetration testers using tools such Ncrack [31]. The system ran successfully as designed in all instance where the attackers will reach Honeypots and attempt other exploits.

V. Conclusion

As more commercial and critical services and applications are migrating to the cloud infrastructure, it is imperative to design and implement proper controls to defend against external threats. While the underlying technologies for this Honeynet system may already exist, it is a novel attempt to integrate them in such a way that presents a more dynamic, scalable defense solution in the cloud environment.

While the preliminary results are promising, more work is needed to make it a complete solution. Potential future work includes,

- Integration with container introspection software, e.g., Prometheus [32].
- Honeypot for other common attack vectors, e.g., SQL injection.
- Working prototype with other public cloud platforms, e.g., Amazon AWS.

References

[1] L. Columbus, "State of Enterprise Cloud Computing," Forbes, 2018. https://www.forbes.com/sites/louiscolumbus/2018/08/30/state-of-enterprise-cloud-computing-2018/ [retrieved: Jun 2020]

[2] DoD, "DoD Digital Modernization Strategy," Department of Defense, U.S.A., 2019. https://media.defense.gov/2019/Jul/12/2002156622/-1/-1/1/DOD-DIGITAL-MODERNIZATION-STRATEGY-2019.PDF [retrieved: Jun 2020]

[3] Congressional Research Service, "DOD's Cloud Strategy and the JEDI Cloud Procurement," 2019. https://fas.org/sgp/crs/natsec/IF11264.pdf [retrieved: Jun 2020]

[4] N. Afshan, "Analysis and Assessment of the Vulnerabilities in Cloud Computing," International Journal of Advanced Research in Computer Science, vol. 8, no. 2, 2017.

[5] M. Rani and Gagandeep, "A Review of Intrusion Detection System in Cloud Computing," in proceedings International Conference on Sustainable Computing in Science, Technology & Management (SUSCOM 2019), pp. 770-776, 2019.

[6] F. Cohen, "The Deception Toolkit," Risks Digest vol. 19, 1998.

[7] DoD, "Department of Defense Cloud Computing Security Requirement Guide," Defense Information Systems Agency, U.S.A., 2017. https://rmf.org/wp-content/uploads/2018/05/Cloud_Computing_SRG_v1r3.pdf [retrieved: Jun 2020]

[8] C. K. Ng, L. Pan, and Y. Xiang, "Honeypot Frameworks and Their Applications: A New Framework," Springer Briefs on Cyber Security Systems and Networks, 2018.

[9] S. Krishnaveni, S. Prabakaran, and S. Sivamohan, "A Survey on Honeypot and Honeynet Systems for Intrusion Detection in Cloud Environment," Journal of Computational and Theoretical Nanoscience, vol. 15, pp. 2949-2935, 2018.

[10] L. Spitzner, "The Honeynet Project: Trapping the Hackers," IEEE Security & Privacy, vol. 1, no. 2, pp. 15-23, 2003.

[11] L. Spitzner, "Honeypot Farms," Symantec, 2003. https://www.symantec.com/connect/articles/honeypot-farms [retrieved: Jun 2020]

[12] R. Bertheir, "HoneyBrid: Combining Low and High Interaction Honeypots," Honeynet, 2009. https://www.honeynet.org/2009/05/27/honeybrid-combining-low-and-high-interaction-honeypots/ [retrieved: Jun 2020]

[13] W. Han, Z. Zhao, A. Doupe, and G. J. Ahn, "HoneyMix: Toward SDN-based Intelligent Honeynet," in proceedings 2016 ACM International Workshop on Security in Software Defined Networks & Network Function Virtualization (SDN-NFV Security '16), pp. 1-6, 2016.

[14] S. Kyung et al., "HoneyProxy: Design and implementation of next-generation honeynet via SDN," In proceedings 2017 IEEE Conference on Communications and Network Security (CNS 2017), pp. 1-9, 2017.

[15] S. Ravji and M. Ali, "Integrated Intrusion Detection and Prevention System with Honeypot in Cloud Computing," in proceedings 2018 International Conference on Computing, Electronics & Communications Engineering (iCCECE), pp. 95-100, 2018.

[16] P. A. Pandire and V. B. Gaikwad, "Attack Detection in Cloud Virtual Environment and Prevention using Honeypot," in proceedings of the International Conference on Inventive Research Applications (ICIRCA 2018), pp. 515-520, 2018.

[17] C. Polska, "Proactive Detection of Security incidents: Honeypots," ENISA, Tech. Rep., 2012.

[18] Dionaea, http://dionaea.carnivore.it/ [retrieved: Jun 2020]

[19] Honeyd, http://www.honeyd.org/ [retrieved: Jun 2020]

[20] Kippo, https://github.com/desaster/kippo/ [retrieved: Jun 2020]

[21] Glastopf, http://glastopf.org/ [retrieved: Jun 2020]

[22] H. Gjermundrod and I. Dionysiou, "CloudHoneyCY - An Integrated Honeypot Framework for Cloud Infrastructures," in proceedings 2015 IEEE/ACM 8th International Conference on Utility and Cloud Computing, pp. 630-635, 2015.

[23] V. Singh and S. K. Pandey, "Revisiting Cloud Security Threat: Dictionary Attack," in proceedings of International Conference on Advancements in Computing & Management (ICACM 2019), pp. 175-180, 2019.

[24] S. Sentanoe, B. Taubmann, and H. P. Reiser, "Virtual Machine Introspection Based SSH Honeypot," in proceedings of the 4th Workshop on Security in Highly Connected IT Systems (SHCIS'17), pp. 13-18, 2017.

[25] N. Majithia, "Honey-System: Design, Implementation and Attack Analysis," PhD Thesis, Indian Institute of Technology, Kanpur, 2017.

[26] M. N. Khandhar and M. S. Shah, "Docker-The Future of Virtualization," International Journal of Research and Analytical Reviews, 6(2), pp. 164–167, 2019.

[27] T. Watts, R. G. Benton, W. B. Glisson, and J. Shropshire, "Insight from a Docker Container Introspection," in proceedings of the 52nd Hawaii International Conference on System Sciences (HICSS 2019), pp. 7194-7203, 2019.

[28] J. Uitto, S. Rauti, S. Laurén, and V. Leppänen, "A Survey on Anti-honeypot and Anti-Introspection Methods," Recent Advances in Information Systems and Technologies. WorldCIST 2017. Advances in Intelligent Systems and Computing, vol. 570, Springer, 2017.

[29] N. Krawetz, "Anti-Honeypot Technology," IEEE Security & Privacy, vol. 2, no. 1, pp. 76-79, 2004.

[30] K. R. Sekar, V. Gayathri, G. Anisha, K. S. Ravichandran, and R. Manikandan, "Dynamic Honeypot Configuration for Intrusion Detection," in proceedings 2nd International Conference on Trends in Electronics and Informatics (ICOEI 2018), pp. 1397-1401, 2018.

[31] Ncrack, https://nmap.org/ncrack/ [retrieved: Jun 2020]

[32] Prometheus, https://prometheus.io/ [retrieved: Jun 2020]

On Business Models for Vehicle-to-Everything Systems Based on 5G Slicing

Eugen Borcoci, Marius Vochin, Serban Georgica Obreja
University POLITEHNICA of Bucharest - UPB
Bucharest, Romania
Emails: eugen.borcoci@elcom.pub.ro, marius.vochin@upb.ro, serban@radio.pub.ro

***Abstract*—Vehicle-to-Everything (V2X) and Internet of Vehicles are complex multi-actor systems offering to vehicles capabilities to exchange data with other entities (vehicles, infrastructure, grid, pedestrians, etc.) The V2X services aim to improve the transport, safety and comfort on the roads and also to help autonomous driving. The 5G technology can provide a powerful support for V2X, in multi-tenant, multi-domain, multi-operator and end-to-end contexts. Particularly, the 5G slicing technology is able to construct dedicated slices, to serve V2X needs. The complexity of the V2X systems and the multitude of visions led to proposal of many variants of V2X business models and ecosystems, comprising several cooperating actors. The business models are important, given that they essentially determines the requirements and architectures; for V2X systems and is still an open research topic. This work in progress attempts to analyze some relevant business models for 5G slicing and discuss how they can be adapted for rich V2X environment. The paper can help the reader to understand what are the possible stakeholders sets in the V2X complex environment, their interactions and to define the architecture followed by the design of a particular V2X system.**

Keywords—Vehicle-to-Everthing; 2X; 5G slicing; Business models; Stakeholders; Management and Orchestration; Software Defined Networking; Network Function Virtualization; Service management.

I. INTRODUCTION

The Vehicle-to-Everything (V2X) communications and services include many use cases in single or multi-tenancy, multi-operator and multi-domain contexts. Consequently, different sets of service requirements exist, e.g., from enhanced real-time navigation systems on board, to a self-automated car, or a video streaming played on the in-vehicle infotainment system.

The basic vehicular communications have covered essentially vehicle-to-vehicle (V2V) and vehicle-to-road/infrastructure (V2R/V2I) communications. Recently, extended models and services are included in the V2X umbrella, like: vehicle-to-pedestrian (V2P) - direct communication, vehicle-to-vulnerable road user (VRU), vehicle-to-network (V2N) - including cellular networks and Internet, Vehicle to sensors (V2S), vehicle-to-power grid (V2G) and vehicle-to-home (V2H).

V2X allows vehicles to directly communicate with each other, to roadside infrastructure, and to other road users for the benefit of better road safety, traffic efficiency, smart mobility, environmental sustainability, and driver convenience. V2X contributes to fully autonomous driving development through its unique non-line-of-sight sensing capability which allows vehicles to detect potential hazards, traffic, and road conditions from longer distances. Typical use cases and services/applications for V2X comprise: active road safety applications (including autonomous driving); warnings, notifications, assistance; traffic efficiency and management applications; infotainment applications. Therefore, IoV extends the traditional basic functions like vehicles driving and safety to novel target domains such as enhanced traffic management, automobile production, repair and vehicle insurance, road infrastructure construction and repair, logistics and transportation, etc.

Internet of Vehicles (IoV) is an extension of the V2X, aiming to create a global network of vehicles – enabled by various *Wireless Access Technologies* (WAT) [1][2]. It involves the Internet and includes heterogeneous access networks. IoV can be seen as a special use case of *Internet of Things* (IoT); however, IoV contains intelligent "terminals" such as vehicles (maybe some of them - autonomous). The complexity of the V2X/IoV claims for a strong support infrastructure. The 5G slicing technology is considered to be an appropriate candidate.

The 5G mobile network technologies offer powerful features, in terms of capacity, speed, flexibility and services, to answer the increasing demand and challenges addressed to communication systems and Internet [3]-[5]. 5G can provide specific types of services to simultaneously satisfy various customer/tenant demands in a multi-x fashion (the notation –x stands for: tenant, domain, operator and provider).

The 5G network slicing concept (based on virtualization and softwarization) enables programmability and modularity for network resources provisioning, adapted to different vertical service requirements (in terms of bandwidth, latency, mobility, etc.) [6]-[9]. In a general view, a *Network Slice* (NSL) is a managed logical group of subsets of resources, organized as virtual dedicated networks, isolated from each other (w.r.t. performance and security), but sharing the same infrastructure. The NSLs functionalities are implemented by Physical/Virtual network functions (PNFs/VNFs), chained in graphs, in order to compose services dedicated to different sets of users. The slices are programmable and have the ability to expose their capabilities to the users. The actual run-time execution entities are instantiated slices, whose life cycles are controlled by the management and control entities belonging to the *Management, Orchestration and Control Plane (MO&C)*. The *Network Function Virtualization* (NFV)[10]-[13] and *Software Defined Networks* (SDN) technologies can cooperate [14] to manage, orchestrate and control the 5G sliced environment, in a flexible and programmable way. The 3GPP [4][5] has defined three fundamental categories of 5G slice scenarios: *Massive machine type communication (mMTC); Ultra reliability low latency communication (URLLC); Enhanced mobile broadband (eMBB).*

The 5G slicing is considered to be a strong candidate to fulfill the requirements of V2X systems. Several studies and projects deal with development of V2X systems based on 5G sliced infrastructure; some examples are [15]-[19]. The dedicated 5G slices can provide the required capabilities for multiple tenants, while working over a 5G shared infrastructure. However, it is recognized [15][16], that the heterogeneous and complex features of V2X services neither allow the straightforward mapping of them onto basic reference slice types – like eMBB, URLLC and mMTC services, nor the mapping into a single V2X slice. Additional customization is necessary in order to create V2X dedicated slices.

The V2X/IoV systems are highly complex, involving several technical and organizational entities which cooperate in a business *ecosystem*. Generally, a business ecosystem is a network of organizations/stakeholders such as suppliers, distributors, customers, competitors, government agencies, etc., involved in the delivery of a specific product or service through both competition and cooperation. The entities/stakeholders/actors interact with each other, in order to achieve together the goals of the system. An equivalent term is *Business Model* (BM) to define the set of stakeholders and their interactions.

In a V2X ecosystem new actors are involved, besides traditional Internet and network/service providers or operators. These new actors could be road authorities, municipalities, regulators and vehicle manufacturers *Original Equipment Manufacturers* (OEM).

The development of the 5G complex sliced systems supposes to initially define the BMs, which essentially determines the roles and responsibilities of the entities and then the system requirements and architecture. This need is equally true for V2X systems and today it is still an open research topic. Concerning V2X BMs, it is recognized (see 5G PPP Automotive Working Group, Business Feasibility Study for 5G V2X Deployment [22]) that there is still some lack of insights into the required rollout conditions, roles of different stakeholders, investments, business models and expected profit from *Connected and Automated Mobility* (CAM) services. On the other side, the general BMs for 5G sliced networks should be adapted and refined in order to well serve the V2X system's needs.

Considering the above reasons, this work in progress attempts to analyze some relevant BMs for 5G slicing and discuss how they can be adapted for V2X environment. Due to space limitation, this text cannot afford to offer detailed explanations about the BMs presented; the objective is to identify the major points of similarity of different BMs for 5G slicing, then 5G-V2X approaches and to study their possible mapping. The paper contribution is mainly an overview and comparison of different solutions.

The paper structure is described below. Section II outlines the stakeholder roles in 5G slicing, given that such definitions determine essentially the overall system architecture. Section III refines the general BMs to be adapted to 5G V2X communications and services. Section IV performs an analysis of some factors that lead to different V2X-5G business models. Section VI summarizes conclusions and future work.

II. Business Model and Stakeholder Roles in 5G Slicing

The objective of this section is to present a few relevant BMs proposed for 5G sliced systems and to identify the main roles of actors, in order to prepare their customization for V2X case in the next section. The layered architecture of the 5G slicing strongly depends on the stakeholder roles defined by the BM. Different BMs have been proposed, aiming to support multi-tenant, multi-domain end-to-end (E2E) and multi-operator capabilities in various contexts. Several examples are summarized below.

A. Example 1

A basic model (see A. Galis, [7]) defines four main roles:

End User (EU): consumes (part of) the services supplied by the slice tenant, without providing them to other business actors.

Slice Tenant (SLT): is the generic user of a specific slice, including network/cloud/data centers, which can host customized services. A SLT can request from a *Network Slice Provider* (NSLP) to create a new slice instance dedicated to support some SLT specific services. The SLT can lease virtual resources from one or more NSLPs in the form of a virtual network, where the tenant can realize, manage and then provide *Network Services* (NS) to its individual end users. A NS is a composition of *Network Functions (NFs),* defined in terms of the individual NFs and the mechanism used to connect them. A single tenant may define and run one or several slices in its domain.

Network Slice Provider (NSLP): can be typically a telecommunication service provider (owner or tenant of the infrastructures from which network slices are constructed). The NSLP can construct multi-tenant, multi-domain slices, on top of infrastructures offered by one or several InPs.

Infrastructure Provider (InP): owns and manages the physical infrastructure (network/cloud/data centre). It could lease its infrastructure (as it is) to a slice provider, or it can itself construct slices (the BM is flexible) and then lease the infrastructure in network slicing fashion.

Note that the scope of the above model is limited; it is operational only, i.e., it does not detail all external entities of the overall ecosystem, which may have strong impact on the operational model, e.g., Standards Developing Organizations (SDOs), policy makers, etc.

An important feature of the above BM is its recursive capability (see Ordonez et al., [8]); a tenant can at its turn, to offer parts of its sliced resources to other tenants, and so on.

B. Example 2

A recent document of the 5G-PPP Architecture Working Group [4] describes a more refined BM:

Service Customer (SC): uses services offered by a Service Provider (SP). The vertical industries are considered as typical examples of SCs.

Service Provider (SP): it has a generic role, comprising three possible sub-roles, depending on the service offered to the SC: *Communication SP* offers traditional telecom services; *Digital SP* offers digital services (e.g., enhanced mobile broadband and IoT to various verticals); *Network Slice as a Service (NSLaaS) Provider* offers a NSL and its services. The SPs have to design, build and operate high-level services, using aggregated network services.

Network Operator (NOP): orchestrates resources, potentially offered by multiple *virtualized infrastructure providers* (VISP). The NOP uses aggregated virtualized infrastructure services to design, build, and operate network services that are offered to SPs.

Virtualization Infrastructure SP (VISP): offers virtualized infrastructure services and designs, builds, and operates virtualization infrastructure(s) (i.e., networking and computing resources). Sometimes, a VISP offers access to a variety of resources by aggregating multiple technology domains and making them accessible through a single *Application Programming Interface* (API).

Data Center SP (DCSP): designs, builds, operates and offers data center services. A DCSP differs from a VISP by offering "raw" resources (i.e., host servers) in rather centralized locations and simple services for consumption of these raw resources.

The hierarchy of this model (in the top-down sense of a layered architecture) is: SC, SP, NOP, VISP, DCSP. Note that in practice, a single organization can play one or more roles of the above list.

Several recent Public Private Partnership (PPP) Phase I/II collaborative research are running, having as objectives 5G technologies (see several examples in [A. Galis, [7]). Some of them extended the list of role definitions, to allow various possible customer-provider relationships between verticals, operators, and other stakeholders.

C. Example 3

The 5G-MoNArch European project [20] proposes an ecosystem model for 5G slicing. The *Mobile network operators (MNOs)* will change from a vertically integrated model, where they own the spectrum, antenna and core network sites and equipment, to a layered model where each layer might be managed or implemented by a different stakeholder. A stakeholder is defined in [20] as an individual, entity or organisation that affects how the overall system operates. The MoNArch stakeholder roles [20] are:

End User: the ultimate entity which uses the services provides by a Tenant or the MSP.

Tenant: purchases and utilizes a network slice and its associated services offered by a *Mobile Service Provider (MSP)*. Tenant examples are: *Mobile Virtual Network Operator (*MVNO), enterprise or any entity that requires telecommunications services for its business operations.

Mobile Service Provider (MSP): is the main entity which provides mobile internet connectivity and telecommunication services to its users. To this aim, the MSP constructs *network slices* and their function chains to compose services. Examples of slices can be eMBB or mMTC. The MSP set of tasks are: design, building offering and operation of its services.

Infrastructure Provider (InP): owns and manages the network infrastructure (antennas, base stations, remote radio heads, data centers, etc.), and offers it to the MSP, in the form of *Infrastructure-as-a-Service* (IaaS).

In practice a larger organizational entiy could exist, i.e., *Mobile Network Operator (MNO)* which operates and owns the mobile network, *combining the roles of MSP and InP*.

The Monarch model further refines the roles of some entities which can exist, as distinct actors:

Virtualisation Infrastructure Service Provider (VISP) may exist, as an intermediate actor between InP and MSP. It designs, builds and operates a virtualization infrastructure on top of the InP services, and offers its infrastructure service to the MSP.

At a lower logical level, an *NFV Infrastructure (NFVI) supplier* may exist, to provide a NFV infrastructure to its customers, i.e., to the VISP and/or directly to the MSP.

TABLE I. BUSINESS MODELS FOR 5G SLICING

Relevant business models examples			
Basic Model [7]	***5G-PPP [4]***	***MoNArch project [20]***	
End User (EU)	Service Customer (SC)	End User Tenant	
Slice Tenant (SLT)	Service Provider (SP) (offers slices)	Mobile Service Provider (MSP) - can belong to MNO	
Network SliceProvider (NSLP)	Network Operator (NOP) (offers ggregated services)	Virtualisation Infrastructure Service Provider (VISP) – can belong to MNO	VNF supplier (it can be a separate entity)
Infrastructure Provider (InP) Hardware supplier		NFV Infrastructure (NFVI) supplier	
	Virtualization Infrastructure SP (VISP)	Infrastructure Provider (InP)	
	Data Center SP (DCSP)	Hardware supplier	

A *VNF supplier* may also exist to offer virtualized software (SW) components to the MSP.

The last but not least is the *Hardware (HW) supplier* which offers hardware to the InPs (server, antenna, cables, etc.).

D. Example 4

The document 3GPP TR22.830 [21] defines a 5G business model. It is shown that 5G opens the door to new BM roles for 3rd parties, allowing them more control of system capabilities. 5G Three role models are envisaged in 5G for stakeholders: a. The MNO owns and manages both the access and core network; b. An MNO owns and manages the core network, the access network is shared among multiple operators (i.e., RAN sharing); c. Only part of the network is owned and/or managed by the MNO, with other parts being owned and/or managed by a 3rd party.

Note that the above different models cannot be exactly on-to-one mapped, given the different contexts and visions and also the degree of splitting into sub-modules. However, a general equivalence can be observed (see TABLE 1). Here, we consider the basic model the most orthogonal one.

III. Business Models for 5G V2X

The key technology enablers for 5G V2X communication and services are currently studied and understood in the wireless industry and standardization of 3GPP Release 16 V2X is in its final phase [22]. Apart from traditional vehicular services, it is forecasted that advanced CAM services (e.g., high-definition (HD) maps support, highway chauffeur, tele-operated driving, platooning, fully autonomous driving, extended sensors, etc.) will be enabled through next-generation 5G V2X starting with 3GPP Release 16. This section will provide two examples of BMs/ecosystems for 5G V2X.

The 5G PPP Automotive Working Group [23] has defined a general 5G V2X BM, capturing not only operational features but also business relationships. It identified the following key stakeholder categories involved in the deployment of 5G V2X technologies: *5G industry* (network operators, network and devices vendors), *automotive industry*, *Standards Developing Organizations* (SDOs), *road infrastructure operators, policy makers* and *users*. The interactions between them are shown in Figure 1.

5G industry: include any general business activity or commercial enterprise developing or using 5G or providing 5G-related services, e.g., *MNOs, Telecom vendors, Cloud providers*, device providers, software developers, etc.

Automotive Industry (AutoIn): includes car *Original Equipment Manufacturer (OEMs)* (e.g., car manufacturers), component manufacturers, Tier 1 suppliers, CAM service providers, HD map providers and other automotive-specific technology providers (it can also include other services such as the logistic sectors). This category brings the automotive expertise and services (including mobility services) to customers (business and consumers).

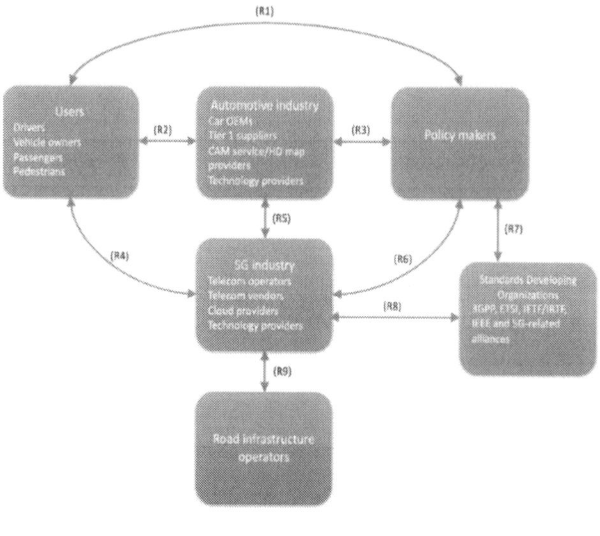

Figure 1. The main stakeholders and relationships in the context of 5G V2X deployment [23]

Standard Development Organizations (SDO): 3rd Generation Partnership Project (3GPP), European Telecommunications Standards Institute (ETSI), Internet Engineering Task Force (IETF), Internet Research Task Force (IRTF), Institute of Electrical and Electronics Engineers (IEEE) and 5G-related alliances such as Next Generation Mobile Networks (NGMN), Industrial Internet Consortium (IIC), 5G Automotive Association (5GAA) and Automotive Edge Computing Consortium (AECC). For safety-related 5G applications (e.g. *Advanced Driver Assistance Systems* - ADAS and autonomous driving), pertinent standards developing organizations such as International Organization for Standardization (ISO) may be also relevant players.

Road Infrastructure Operators (RIO): national or regional entities (public/private) performing deployment, operation and maintenance of physical road infrastructure. They may also manage road traffic operations, own or operate the toll system, etc.

Policy Makers (PM): provide the highest authorities and regulate the relationships within the whole stakeholder ecosystem, including 5G industry, automotive industry, SDOs and users. They are international or national government authorities or organizations defining the legal framework and policies, such as road and transport authorities or telecom regulators. The ITU as well as national spectrum regulators belong to this category.

Users: drivers, vehicle owners, passengers or pedestrian.

The detailed description of the interactions between the stakeholders is given in the 5G PPP Automotive Working Group document [23]. Shortly, the interactions are:

R1 (Users- PMs): to provide to the users the authority regulation to be followed (e.g., for environmental, safety and financial aspects).

R2 (Users - Automotive Industry): to collect feedback from users in order to define the requirements and features of the new products, functionalities and services.

R3 (PMs– AutoIn): PMs define the regulation framework to be followed by AutoIn, while the latter provides feedback to the PMs to support definitions and improvement of regulations.

R4 (Users - 5G Industry): Users buy products and services from the 5G Industry. The latter collects feedback used as inputs to define the network requirements, in terms of Quality of Experience (QoE), and user needs for services and new applications.

R5 (AutoIn - 5G Industry): for inter – cooperation, allowing design a 5G V2X technology to meet the system and component level needs. The AutoIn defines the network requirements for their products and services; the 5G Industry should fulfill the functionality and performance requirements.

R6 (PMs - 5G Industry): PMs define the regulations that the 5G Industry must follow. The latter gives feedback to the PMs to influence the definition of new regulations.

R7 (PMs -SDO): SDOs have to consider regulatory conditions in standards development (e.g., ETSI work is regulated by the of the EU Commission).

R8 (SDO - 5G Industry): The SDOs define the standards to be implemented in the 5G deployments. E.g., for autonomous driving applications ultrareliable low latency are needed, based on safety standards.

R9 (5G Industry - RIO): RIO may participate in the deployment of 5G V2X and provide or facilitate licenses or other infrastructure requirements that are under their responsibility (PMs are also involved here). RIO may define network requirements for the 5G Industry. The 5G Industry shall offer communication services to the RIO based on commercial agreements. However, it is expected that 5G network providers will own and operate most or parts of the network infrastructure. A subset of actors out of the general model will cooperate within the *operational BM*, i.e.: 5G Industry, Automotive industry, users, and possibly - road infrastructure operators. However, the policy makers, SDOs and road infrastructure operators strongly influence the requirements and also the architecture of the V2X systems, as presented above in interaction description.

Usually, 5G network providers will own and operate most or parts of the network infrastructure. This entity can be split into RAN infrastructure provider (offering the physical infrastructure, e.g., antenna sites and the hardware equipment) and cloud infrastructure provider (it owns and manages local and central data centers providing the virtual resources, such as computing, storage and networking). In practice, the roles of 5G network providers can be taken by the MNOs, but is possible that Road Infrastructure Operators deploys or operate (parts of) the 5G V2X network, directly providing the necessary coverage for CAM services to the users.

The network deployment investment can be done by a single actor, called network operator (e.g., a traditional MNO). However, the model in Figure 1 is general, in the sense that potentially any actor (e.g., a road operator) could invest in network deployment.

The project 5GCAR [24]-[26] identifies a BM similar to that developed by 5G PPP Automotive Working Group. In the operational scenarios the following actors can interact: *5G Industry, Automotive industry, Road Infrastructure Operators* and *users.* Those stakeholders may assume different roles identified in the application of the network slicing feature:

Tenant entity: rents and leverages 5G connectivity. Note that Road operator, OEMs or other organization may also have this role.

Mobile Service Provider (MSP): provides to different tenants 5G, dedicated slices for customized services.

The 5G infrastructure providers (5GInP): can be divided into cloud and RAN providers; they offer the elements needed for the MSP to implement the slices.

Non-V2X (supplementary) service provider: can provide passenger targeted services such as enhanced infotainment, mobile office, etc.

The other entities presented in the general BM (Figure1), i.e., Policy makers, SDOs, influence indirectly the system requirements and specifications of the operational BM. It can be seen that the general basic 5G slicing operational BM (see Example 1) can be mapped approximately one-to-one onto the V2X operational BM.

IV. The Heterogeneity of 5G V2X Business Models

This section will summarize the factors leading to heterogeneity in the area of 5G V2X BMs and also affecting the particular architectures. Note that, given the topics complexity, this analysis cannot be exhaustive; some aspects are not touched, or only briefly mentioned.

A major factor which leads to many variants of BMs is the multitude of real-life players which can be active (directly or indirectly) in the 5G V2X system assembly and also the variety of V2X applications/services. Actors providing key services for the automotive sector can be split in two categories: service providers of enabling platforms, which manage the data and allow services to be built on top of the data; connectivity providers, which construct and manage connectivity facilities over cellular networks. Inside each category several types of actors can be included.

A non-exhaustive list of actors comprises:

Connectivity Players (MNOs, Transport Services Providers, (TSPs), ICT Solution & Cloud Platform Providers, Intelligent Transportation System (ITS));

Automotive OEMs (Cars, Trucks);

Suppliers (Tier 1 & 2 (System Integrators), Wireless Module Vendors, Chipset Vendors, Software/Solutions, Middleware, Over the Top Services Providers (OTT), Connectivity/ Bluetooth, Databases, etc.);

Application platforms (Software - based, Fleet/ Commercial, Autonomous Driving, Smartphone Platforms);

Business Users (Public Transport, Company Fleets, Freight, Car Rental, Taxi Fleets, Delivery systems, Emergency Response systems);

Consumers (End user consumers, Families, Small Office Home Office (SoHo);

Application types (Mobility as a Service, Maps & NavigationTelematics / Tracking, Communications Safety & Maintenance, Media & Entertainment, Productivity).

Besides the above, *additional stakeholders* can play specific roles: Insurance, Dealers, Auto Repair, Regulatory Bodies, Local Authorities (Government, Law Enforcement, Smart City, Road Operators), Location-based commerce players, Security infrastructure and services providers.

The forecasts estimate that new actors will enter the auto industry (increase more than 45% by 2030, [27]). Therefore, in order to create a clear and stable ecosystem, the actors' roles/activities and interactions, should be defined. Cooperation is necessary: telecom operators will provide their infrastructure and licensed spectrum; the automotive suppliers will create the chips and sensors compatible with the technology. So, the typical value chain is transformed into a complex ecosystem; actors will share a part of knowledge and resources. The competition will exist and influence the ecosystem structure. From the above reasons, some relationships between possible actors are still uncertain today.

In [26][27], several variants of 5G V2X ecosystems are defined. In each one, a single actor provides the platform, e.g.: MNO, OEM, Automotive Supplier (AS), etc. Interactions between some of actors are established based on Service Level Agreements (SLA).

There are also other lower level technical factors, determining the heterogeneity of 5G V2X BMs and architectures for slicing solutions. The management, orchestration and control subsystem is directly involved within these aspects. Some examples of such factors are given below.

The *services deployment* is inherently heterogeneous, depending on applications to be supported. An example is the traffic locality property (at the edge of the network/slice or crossing the core part). An orchestrator should be aware of such traffic properties and, if necessary, deploy the corresponding network functions at the mobile edge. The orchestrator needs to have enough topology information of slices in order to be able to install appropriate functions at right places. The type of vehicular applications and services will determine the degree of pushing to the edge some functions.

The classical principle of *vertical separation of services* in *network-related* (i.e., connectivity–oriented) and *application-level services* (e.g., caching, video transcoding, content-oriented, web server, etc.) could be preserved or not. The separation will require, respectively one orchestrator vs. separate network/service orchestrators. One can speak about *segregated* or *integrated* orchestration, respectively. Concerning slicing, one can define some slices offering essentially connectivity services and other dedicated to high-level applications. The clear separation of areas of responsibility over resources could be an advantage for operational stability (e.g., a segregated RAN orchestrator could still maintain basic RAN services even if an application-oriented orchestrator fails). On the other hand, the integrated orchestration could be attractive, in particular for operators, if both kinds of services could be orchestrated in the same fashion (and possibly even with the same orchestration infrastructure). These two options also determine heterogeneity at M&O architectural level.

Segregated orchestrators lead to a more complex overall architecture. One must assign areas of responsibilities from a resource perspective (which orchestrator controls - what resources); one should identify services pertaining to each orchestrator. The split of service is also a problem, i.e., the service description should define the "network" and "application-facing" parts of the service. Aligning the control decisions taken by these two kinds of orchestrators in a consistent way is also not trivial. In an integrated orchestration approach, all these problems disappear. However, an integrated orchestrator might be very complex if required to treat substantially different services (one-size-fits-all orchestration approach is rather not the best choice).

An integrated orchestrator is a more challenging piece of software (from both dependability and performance perspectives) but would result in a simpler overall architecture. Considering the above rationale, we defend the idea that from the slicing point of view, a segregate orchestrator is a better choice. However, in practice, both approaches have been pursued in different projects. Currently, a final verdict commonly agreed, on segregated versus integrated orchestration is not yet available. Apparently, there is no need to standardize this option, as long as both of them could be realized inside a meta-architecture. So, for the time being, we can state that M&O heterogeneity, from this point of view, will last.

Another architectural choice is on *"flat"* or *"hierarchical"* orchestration. In the flat solution, a single instance of a particular orchestrator type is in charge of all assigned resources. In the hierarchical solution, there are multiple orchestrators (a "hierarchical" model is needed, when orchestrators know to talk to each other). Note that a hierarchical orchestrator is *not necessarily* a segregated one, because all hierarchy members could deal with the same type of services.

Multi-tenant, multi-domain, multi-operator context of the planned 5G V2X system will influence the BM, making necessary to split the responsibilities among actors, for both categories: high level services and connectivity ones. *Multi-domain scenarios* create new problems [28] (e.g., in the case of a multi-domain "federated" slice). In a flat model, each orchestrator of a domain is actually multi-orchestration capable, i.e., it can discuss/negotiate with other domains' orchestrators. In the hierarchical model, a higher-level orchestrator could exist, in charge of harmonizing multiple organizations cooperation. However, several issues are not fully solved today: which entity would run that multi-domain orchestrator, trust issues, preservation of domains independency, assuring the fairness, etc.

Relationship of the *M&O system* and the 5GT V2X *slicing system* is another factor of BM architectural variability, depending on what the definition of a slice is. A largely agreed solution is to have a general orchestrator (configured offline), capable to trigger the construction of a new slice and then to install in this new slice its own dedicated orchestrator (before the slice run-time). To still assure the basic services outside any slice (e.g., packet forwarding at network level) one can construct an additional special orchestrator installed outside of all slices. Currently, many combinations have been proposed, and there is still no consensus on such matters. The convergence of solutions will be determined probably by the adoption of a more unique definition of a slice – which could assure better inter-operability.

V. Conclusions and Future Work

This is an overview-type paper; it analyzed several business models/ecosystems for 5G slicing and then those for V2X and discuss how the 5G BM can be adapted for V2X environment. It has been shown that a large variety of proposals exist in various studies, standards and projects, given the multitude of V2X use cases and the rich set of business actors that could be potentially involved. Some major factors determining the heterogeneity of the BMs proposals have been identified in Section IV.

Considering the above analysis, and to conclude this preliminary study, we propose the steps to be followed to start a 5G V2X system development in slicing approach.

First, the V2X set of high level of services (seen from the end user perspectives) to be implemented should be defined among the rich possible ones (see Section IV).

The identification of the set of involved actors and a first assignment of their roles (especially from business/services point of view) is a major step. Here, some actors would provide only indirect actions (Policy Makers, SDOs, local regulators, etc.). Other actors will participate at operational phases (MNOs, OEMs, Service providers - e.g., OTT, Infrastructure providers, etc.) at run-time.

The multi-domain, multi-tenant, multi-operator characteristics of the 5G V2X system should be selected. Definition of interactions between the actors will complete the high-level description of the 5G V2X BM/ecosystem.

The following steps will refine the BM and go to the requirement identification and architectural definition. The main connectivity and processing/storage technologies should be identified. The regulations, standards, etc., to be enforced have to be identified; they will define but also limit the system capabilities and scope. System requirements identification will follow, considering requirements coming from all actors involved in BM.

The 5G V2X slicing solution (for RAN, core and transport part of the network) should be selected. Here, the refinement of the BM is possible (see Table 1). Then, the system architecture (general and layered - functional) has to be defined, allowing further technical refinement of the system design.

Future work can go further to consider more deeply the multi-x aspects, related to the business models and impact of the BM upon the system management orchestration and control for 5G V2X dedicated slices.

Acknowledgment

The work has been partially funded by the Operational Program Human Capital of the Ministry of European Funds through the Financial Agreement 51675/09.07.2019, SMIS code 125125.

References

[1] M. K. Priyan and G. Usha Devi, "A survey on internet of vehicles: applications, technologies, challenges and opportunities", Int. J. Advanced Intelligence Paradigms, Vol. 12, Nos. 1/2, 2019.

[2] C. Renato Storck and F. Duarte-Figueiredo, "A 5G V2X Ecosystem Providing Internet of Vehicles", Sensors 2019, 19,550, doi: 10.3390/s19030550, www.mdpi.com/journal/sensors, [retrieved January, 2020].

[3] N. Panwar, S. Sharma, A. K. Singh 'A Survey on 5G: The Next Generation of Mobile Communication' Elsevier Physical Communication, 4 Nov 2015, http://arxiv.org/pdf/1511.01643v1.pdf

[4] 5G-PPP Architecture Working Group, "View on 5G Architecture", Version 3.0, June, 2019, https://5g-ppp.eu/wp-content/uploads/2019/07/5G-PPP-5G-Architecture-White-Paper_v3.0_PublicConsultation.pdf, [retrieved June, 2019].

[5] 3GPP TS 23.501 V15.2.0 (2018-06), System Architecture for the 5G System; Stage 2, (Release 15)

[6] X. Foukas, G. Patounas, A. Elmokashfi, and M. K. Marina, "Network Slicing in 5G: Survey and Challenges", IEEE Communications Magazine, May 2017, pp. 94-100.

[7] A. Galis, "Network Slicing- A holistic architectural approach, orchestration and management with applicability in mobile and fixed networks and clouds", http://discovery.ucl.ac.uk/10051374/, [retrieved July, 2019].

[8] J. Ordonez-Lucena et al., "Network Slicing for 5G with SDN/NFV: Concepts, Architectures and Challenges", IEEE Communications Magazine, 2017, pp. 80-87, Citation information: DOI 10.1109/MCOM.2017.1600935.

[9] I. Afolabi, T. Taleb, K. Samdanis, A. Ksentini, and H. Flinck, "Network Slicing & Softwarization: A Survey on Principles, Enabling Technologies & Solutions", IEEE Communications Surveys & Tutorials, March 2018, pp. 2429-2453.

[10] ETSI GS NFV 002, "NFV Architectural Framework", V1.2.1, December 2014.

[11] ETSI GS NFV-IFA 009, "Network Functions Virtualisation (NFV); Management and Orchestration; Report on Architectural Options", Technical Report, V1.1.1, July 2016.

[12] ETSI GR NFV-IFA 028, "Network Functions Virtualisation (NFV) Release 3; Management and Orchestration; Report on architecture options to support multiple administrative domains", Technical Report, V3.1.1, January, 2018.

[13] ETSI GR NFV-EVE 012, Release 3 "NFV Evolution and Ecosystem; Report on Network Slicing Support with ETSI NFV Architecture Framework", Technical Report, V3.1.1, December, 2017.

[14] ONF TR-526, "Applying SDN Architecture to 5G Slicing", April 2016, https://www.opennetworking.org/wp-content/uploads/2014/10/Applying_SDN_Architecture_to_5G_Slicing_TR-526.pdf, [retrieved December, 2019].

[15] A. Molinaro and C. Campolo, "5G for V2X Communications", https://www.5gitaly.eu/2018/wp-

content/uploads/2019/01/5G-Italy-White-eBook-5G-for-V2X-Communications.pdf, [retrieved December, 2019].
[16] S. A. Ali Shah, E. Ahmed, M. Imran, and S. Zeadally, "5G for Vehicular Communications", IEEE Communications Magazine, January 2018, pp.111-117.
[17] K. Katsaros and M. Dianati, "A Conceptual 5G Vehicular Networking Architecture", October 2017, https://www.researchgate.net/publication/309149571, DOI: 10.1007/978-3-319-34208-5_22, [retrieved December 2019].
[18] C. Campolo, A. Molinaro, A. Iera, and F. Menichella, "5G Network Slicing for Vehicle-to-Everything Services", IEEE Wireless Communications, Volume: 24 Issue: 6, DOI: 10.1109/MWC.2017.160040, [retrieved December, 2019].
[19] Friedhelm Ramme, ITS, Transport & Automotive, Ericsson 5G: "From Concepts to Reality" Technology Roadmaps https://5gaa.org/wp-content/uploads/2019/02/Final-Presentation-MWC19-Friedhelm-Ramme-ERICSSON.pdf, [retrieved January, 2020].
[20] H2020-ICT-2016-2, Monarch Project, 5G Mobile Network Architecture for diverse services, use cases and applications in 5G and beyond, Deliverable D2.2, "Initial overall architecture and concepts for enabling innovations", https://5g-monarch.eu/deliverables/ 2018,[retrieved June, 2019].
[21] 3GPP TR 22.830 V16.1.0, TS Group Services and System Aspects, "Feasibility Study on Business Role Models for Network Slicing", (Release 16), 2018 https://itectec.com/archive/3gpp-specification-tr-22-830/ [retrieved May, 2020].
[22] https://www.3gpp.org/release-16.
[23] 5G PPP Automotive Working Group, "Business Feasibility Study for 5G V2X Deployment", https://bscw.5g-ppp.eu/pub/bscw.cgi/d293672/5G%20PPP%20Automotive%20WG_White%20Paper_Feb2019.pdf, [retrieved, January, 2020].
[24] 5GCAR White Paper : Executive Summary, Version: v1.0, 2019-12-10, https://5gcar.eu/wp-content/uploads/2019/12/5GCAR-Executive-Summary-White-Paper.pdf, [retrieved, January 2020].
[25] 5GCAR, Fifth Generation Communication Automotive Research and innovation Deliverable D1.2 5GCAR Mid-Project Report, v1.0 2018-05-31, https://5gcar.eu/wp-content/uploads/2018/08/5GCAR_D1.2_v1.0.pdf, [retrieved, January, 2020].
[26] 5GCAR, Fifth Generation Communication Automotive Research and innovation Deliverable D2.2 "Intermediate Report on V2X Business Models and Spectrum", v2.0, 2019-02-28,https://5gcar.eu/wp-content/uploads/2018/08/5GCAR_D2.2_v1.0.pdf, [retrieved, January, 2020].
[27] B. Martínez de Aragón, J. Alonso-Zarateand, and A. Laya, "How connectivity is transforming the automotive ecosystem". Internet Technology Letters. 2018;1:e14. https://doi.org/10.1001/itl2.14 [retrieved, January, 2020].
[28] Katsalis, N. Nikaein, and A. Edmonds, "Multi-Domain Orchestration for NFV: Challenges and Research Directions", 2016 15th Int'l Conf. on Ubiquitous Computing and Communications and International Symposium on Cyberspace and Security (IUCC-CSS), pp. 189–195, DOI: 10.1109/IUCC-CSS.2016.034, https://ieeexplore.ieee.org/document/7828601, [retrieved July, 2019].

Meshed Trees for Resilient Switched Networks

Peter Willis[1], Nirmala Shenoy[2]
Dept. of Information Sciences and Technologies,
Golisano College of Computing and Information Sciences
Rochester Institute of Technology, Rochester, New York, USA
e-mail: [1]pjw7904@rit.edu, [2]nxsvks@rit.edu

Abstract— **Layer 2 (L2) protocols are fundamental to all network communications. Loop-avoidance in L2 operations is essential for forwarding broadcast frames without them looping throughout network. Loop-avoidance protocols construct a logical tree on the meshed topology, normally used to provide path redundancy in switched networks. Repairing the tree on topology changes results in expensive network downtime and is major challenge faced in L2 networks. In this article, we present the Meshed Tree Protocol (MTP) based on a novel Meshed Tree Algorithm (MTA) as a clean-slate approach to loop avoidance in switched network. MTP leverages the connectivity in the meshed topology to pre-construct several trees from a root. Multiple backup paths are in readiness to takeover in the event of failure of the main path for fast convergence. We limit our work in this article to a comparison of a coded prototype implementation of MTP vs. the Rapid Spanning Tree Protocol (RSTP) in L2 customer networks. The evaluation was conducted on the GENI (Global Environment for Network Innovation) testbed.**

Keywords-Meshed Trees; Pre-constructed Paths; Path Vector VIDs; Hysteresis in Failure Detection.

I. INTRODUCTION

High-performance switched networks are in great demand with the growth in L2 Customer (C), Service Provider (SP) and Backbone Provider (BP) networks. Meshed topologies are adopted in switched networks to provide path redundancy. Consequently, handling of broadcast frames poses a challenge. When a switch receives a broadcast frame on a port it forwards it on all other ports (except the port it was received on). Because there are physical loops in the network due to the meshed topology, this can result in broadcast frames looping in the network infinitely and crashing the network. For this purpose, it is important to forward brought broadcast frames on paths that do not loop. The traditional approach is to construct a logical tree on the physical meshed topology and allow broadcast frames to be forwarded along the tree paths. To construct a logical tree on the switched network, loop avoidance protocols are used. Loop-avoidance protocols use tree algorithms such as Spanning tree and Dijkstra tree to construct the logical tree. Tree algorithms allow construction of a single tree from a root. Hence on a link or switch failure when a tree branch fails, protocols based of these algorithms must reconstruct/repair the tree. As a result, the convergence latency in the event of a network component failure can be high. This is a setback for applications running on switched networks that desire high availability.

Constructing a single logical tree on a meshed topology logically sacrifices the rich path redundancy in the meshed topology. We propose a novel meshed trees algorithm (MTA) that allows construction of multiple trees from a single root. The branches from the multiple trees mesh at the switches thus keeping the redundant paths in readiness and the failover in the event of a (currently used) path failure is immediate. We further propose a novel virtual identifier to pre-construct and maintain the multiple trees. This simplifies the meshed tree protocol implementation significantly, making the protocol lightweight and robust.

In this article, we limit our performance comparison of MTP vs RSTP to highlight the significant performance improvement (several magnitudes) in terms of convergence on link failures that can be achieved with a simple and robust protocol, especially in L2 customer networks. RSTP is a standard protocol and its code is available on the GENI testbed, hence it is readily available to compare the two working prototypes. RSTP also serves as a reference. We collect measurements of an implementation of MTP and RSTP on the GENI testbed [10], for multiple network topologies. A detailed analysis and study of MTP vs RSTP convergence process considering tree construction and recovery on failures, based on message exchanges and port role changes is provided. Several sets of test cases were evaluated. The tree construction process with MTP and RSTP are highlighted and contrasted to explain the difference in operational complexity between the two protocols and to justify the performance improvements with MTP. Future work will cover a study of MTP vs IS-IS based loop-avoidance protocols for L2 SP and BP networks.

The rest of the paper is structured as follows. In Section II, we discuss background work on loop-avoidance protocols, primarily focusing on standards, followed by an introduction to meshed trees. We discuss IS-IS based protocols, the latest loop avoidance protocol standards to address convergence delays experienced by spanning tree protocols, only to highlight their complexity and limitations. We also introduce and compare meshed trees with Dijkstra and spanning trees. Section III describes a meshed trees implementation in a switched network with an example highlighting several of its attributes. Section IV focusses on the performance metrics that will be studied and their significance. Section V provides details on protocol evaluations, and tools and techniques to assess performance. Subsections discuss in detail the performance in three different topologies for multiple test cases. The failures were limited to single link failures and the relative position in the tree which plays an important role in the convergence latency experienced in switched networks. Section VI provides a summary of the results highlighting the significant difference protocol recovery latency and messages among the 2 protocols. Section VII provides a brief conclusion and future work.

II. BACKGROUND

In this section, we present the two major categories of loop avoidance protocols for use in switched networks. Though other alternatives have been proposed we focus on these two categories as they are widely used and serve as a standard for performance comparison. They are:

1. The Spanning Tree Protocol family
2. Dijkstra's Tree Algorithm based Protocols

A. The Spanning Tree Protocol (STP) Family

This includes STP and its faster version – Rapid STP (RSTP), for construction of a single tree in a local area network (LAN). (We limit the discussions in this article to a single LAN). STP has been an IEEE standard since 1998 [8]. In STP, switches exchange Bridge Protocol Data Units (BPDUs) to decide on a logical spanning tree. Roles are assigned to ports so they can allow or block frames. Bridge Medium Access Control (MAC) addresses and port numbers are used to break ties during spanning tree construction. STP recovery process on topology changes result in transients and high recovery delays, as STP uses many timers. RSTP IEEE 802.1w [2] avoids delays incurred due to extensive timer usage by STP and speeds up convergence through fast exchange of proposal and agreement message among switches. RSTP further reduced convergence times by holding a port in readiness if the best port to reach the root bridge (the root port) fails.

B. Dijkstra's Tree Algorithm based Protocols

For high performance networks, such as L2 SP and BP networks, the delays incurred with RSTP were unacceptable. As a consequence, Inter-System Inter-System (IS-IS) based Layer 3 routing solutions that use Dijkstra trees were introduced into L2 operations to improve path and root switch failure resiliency. The IS-IS based solutions construct shortest paths trees from every switch (as a root), to cut down root reelection time. Loop avoidance protocols that use Dijkstra's algorithm are TRILL (Transparent Interconnection of Lots of Links) on RBridges (Router Bridges) [4][5] and Shortest Path Bridging (SPB) [7]. Radia Perlman, the inventor of STP, introduced TRILL [5] as an Internet Engineering Task Force (IETF) effort, as it operates above L2. The TRILL protocol uses the IS-IS routing protocol to take advantage of the numerous trees constructed using Dijkstra's algorithm. Similar to TRILL, SPB, is an IEEE effort that introduced IS-IS link state routing into L2 [7]. Using IS-IS links state routing incurs the following overhead/limitations:

- IS-IS messages are encapsulated in L2 or TRILL messages adding to operational overhead and complexity.
- IS-IS cannot guarantee true loop-freedom; a hop count is included to track and discard looping frames.
- Dijkstra's tree construction is computation intensive [9] and not suited for fast convergence in dynamic networks. During the re-computation time on topology changes, frame delivery is not guaranteed.
- Any link state change must be propagated to all switches, which then wait for a settling time to compute new Dijkstra trees. During this period, frame forwarding is unreliable.
- Reverse congruency requires all switches to compute Dijkstra trees from all other switches, so they can use the same ports in source address tables to forward frames to end devices connected to the other switch. This multiplies the operation complexity and overhead by the number of switches and is a scalability issue.

C. The Need for a New Approach

Current loop-avoidance protocols construct a single logical tree to avoid looping of broadcast frames in meshed networks. This is true for protocols based on spanning trees or on Dijkstra trees. In the event of a single link failure both categories of protocols require dissemination of this information to all switches so they can reconstruct/repair the trees. Repairing trees takes time which is the reason for the convergence latency faced in current loop avoidance protocols. We propose a clean slate approach, which uses Meshed Tree Algorithm that enables construction of multiple trees from a single root.

D. The Meshed Tree Algorithm

Instead of a single spanning tree or shortest path tree as possible with current tree algorithms, MTP [1] adopts a new MTA to compute multiple trees from a root. The multiple paths constructed mesh at the switches and hence are called meshed trees. MTP leverages the connectivity in meshed networks to provision redundant paths from every switch to the root. The redundant paths are in readiness to takeover in the event of a link or main path failure. Maintaining multiple branches would seem to add to the operational complexity, but we use a novel Path Vector virtual ID technique to construct and maintain meshed trees resulting in an extremely light weight protocol, as discussed in Section III.

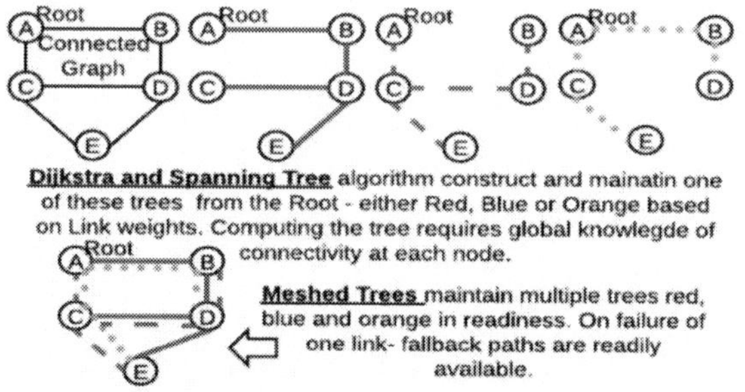

Figure 1. Meshed Trees vs Spanning/Dijkstra Tree

The Meshed Tree Algorithm – is the first of its kind that allows preconstruction of multiple tree branches from a single root. We describe the concept of Meshed trees using Figure 1. In Figure 1, we compare spanning /shortest path tree constructed using Dijkstra and Spanning Tree algorithms to meshed trees. On the top left is a 5-node, 6-edge connected graph. Using either Dijkstra's or Spanning Tree algorithm, one of three trees, i.e. red, blue or orange tree, can be constructed – the outcome is always one tree, from the root node A. The bottom left shows a *meshed tree,* in which all three trees (red, blue and orange) co-exist allowing each node to have multiple paths to the root node A and to reach any other node. In the event a path fails, another path is readily available.

III. The Meshed Tree Protocol

The Meshed Tree Protocol builds fault tolerance in switched networks by computing multiple tree paths from each switch to the root. This ensures that there are alternative paths in readiness on switch or link failures. The number of alternative paths that a switch records can be set as a parameter. MTP computes and maintain these paths with very low overhead and operational complexity using virtual identifiers (VIDs). A VID at a switch identifies a path to the root. A switch acquires and stores multiple VIDs. Hop count is inherent in the VID. VIDs also aid in loop-detection, cutting down on processing time and operational overhead significantly. VIDs are discussed in the Sections below.

A. Meshed Tree Protocol Overview

In this section we explain the construction of meshed trees by MTP in a switched network. We start by designating a root switch it and assigning it a unique VID. Rationale for Root switch designation is discussed next.

1) Root Switch Designation

A switch is designated to be the root. We decided to designate a root to avoid root election delays. However, in the event of failure of this root, we need another root to take over. In spanning tree-based protocols, on the failure of the root, a root election is conducted to elect the next root, subsequent to which the spanning tree is constructed. The root election process incurs heavy delays. Spanning tree protocols, further bias the root election by setting the switch priority such that the switch with higher capacity gets elected as root. This is necessary as the traffic carried by the root switch is significantly higher than other switches. In the case of Dijkstra's algorithm based protocols, every switch is a root, which is an overkill as the number of trees constructed equals the number of switches.

With Mesh Tree Protocol, we designate an optimal number of switches to be roots – one is the primary root, the next is the secondary root and so on. The number of meshed trees constructed equals the number of roots designated. Depending on the network availability needs and based on the services they support, the number of roots can be optimized. The rational for using an optimal set of roots is to avoid root election delay if we used one root, as in spanning tree protocols, and at the same time avoid excessive computations required in computing trees from every switch as with Dijkstra algorithm based protocols. In this article, we restrict our presentation and analysis to a single rooted meshed tree. The goal is to demonstrate fast convergence and quick recovery of broadcast frame forwarding (due to the pre-constructed backup paths) in the event of link failures.

2) Meshed Tree Construction

Meshed trees are constructed and maintained at the switches where the tree information is stored as VIDs. As previously stated, a root is designated and is assigned a VID - say '1'. All other switches acquire VIDs as MTP is executed in the switches. A VID stored at a switch (not the root) is a concatenation of numbers where the first number is the VID of the root. The numbers following the root VID are the port numbers of switches that identify a path to the root. We use a dotted decimal notation for this purpose. For example, a switch – say S1 connected on port 2 of the root switch, will acquire a VID of 1.2. A switch S2 connected on port 3 of switch S1, will acquire a VID of 1.2.3 where the VID 1.2.3 defines the path from switch S2 to the root via switch S1. We next describe the process of using VIDs to define multiple tree paths from every switch to the root using an example 5-switch network.

We use Figure 2 to explain meshed tree construction in a 5- switch network. Figure 2A shows the 5-switch topology. Switch port numbers are noted besides each switch. In Figure 2B, a pink logical tree starting at the root and reaching all switches is shown. We now walk through the process of how the pink logical tree was constructed. The tree construction begins from the root. The root offers (through an advertisement) VID 1.1 on port 1 (appending the outgoing port number 1 to its VID 1). Switch S1 that receives this offer accepts and joins the pink tree by storing VID 1.1. Next, S1 offers VID 1.1.2 to S3 on its port 2. S3 offers VID 1.1.2.2 to S2, and 1.1.2.3 to S4 (as S2 is connected at port 2, and S4 at port 3, of S3). VIDs 1, 1.1, 1.1.2, 1.1.2.2, 1.1.2.3 define the pink logical tree.

In Figure 2C, a similar procedure is used to build the orange tree, from the Root via switch S2 and this tree is defined by VIDs 1, 1.2, 1.2.2, 1.2.3, 1.2.2.1. Figure 2D shows how both trees, are maintained at the switches by *simply storing both sets of VIDs*.

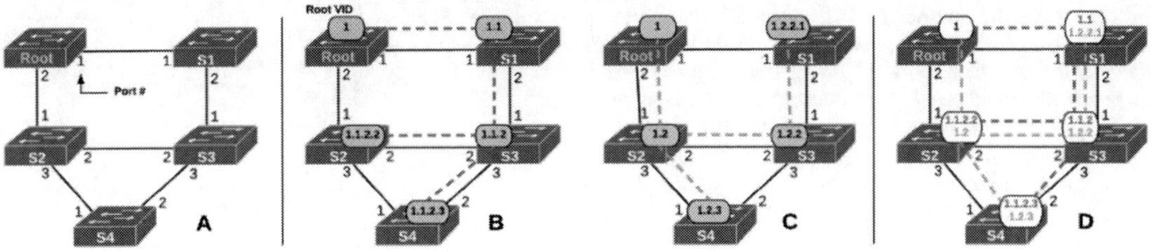

Figure 2. Meshed Trees in Switched Networks

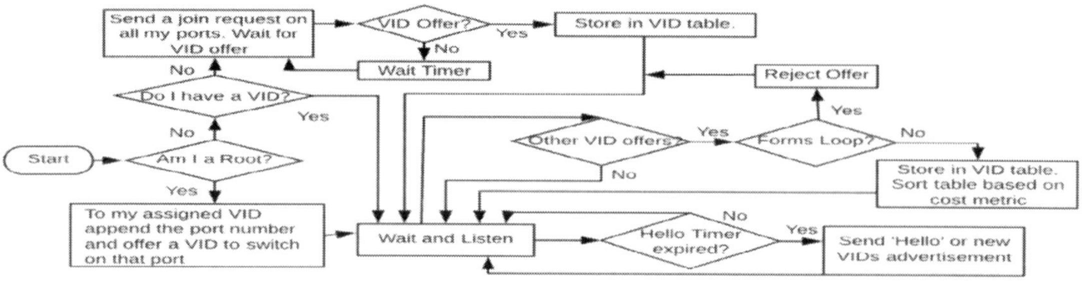

Figure 3. Flow Chart for Simplified Meshed Tree Construction in Switched Network

MTP uses messages that advertise VIDs, and a switch that accepts a VID informs the upstream switch of the VIDs it accepts. We do not include the protocol implementation details in this article, but restrict our presentation to its operations. On startup as only the root switch has a VID, switches that do not have a VID will issue a join-request message on their ports. Figure 3 is a flow chart used at the switches to construct meshed trees.

When MTP is started in a switch, the switch first checks if it is designated root. If this is true (it will have an assigned VID), the root will send a VID advertisement on all its ports. The VID advertisement on each port will be different because when advertising its VID it will append the port number on which the VID advertisement will be sent. Switches that are not designated roots will send a join-request to receive VID advertisements from its neighbors. Every switch that acquires a VID will advertise on all other ports except the port on which the VID was acquired. Thus, switches receive multiple VID advertisements and are able to select VIDs based on the path metric and store them in a VID table, in order of preference. Before accepting a VID, switches do a loop check which is explained below. MTP uses the hello timer to keep its neighbors informed about its current active status. Any changes to the VID tables are advertised.

3) Loop Detection and Preemption

We explain loop detection and pre-emption using an example from Figure 2D. Let S3 offer VID 1.1.2.1 to switch S1. S1 compares the offered VID with its current VIDs, 1.1 and 1.2.2.1. Its current VID 1.1 is a *proper prefix* of the offered VID 1.1.2.1, so S1 knows it is its own ancestor in the offered path to the root. S1 thus detects a loop and will not accept this VID. (Note - the number of digits in the VID is direct measure of hop count).

4) The Distributed Approach to Tree Construction

The process of selecting the best set of VIDs is decided by each switch independently based on the advertisements it hears from its neighbors. On receiving multiple VIDs, a switch stores them in order of preference based on hop count, path cost, or any other metric. In this article, hop count is used. To limit the tree meshing and conserve on memory usage the number of VIDs stored by a switch is limited. *The limited number of VID's in this implementation is 3.* The fact that each switch independently decides on the VIDs it stores based on a preference criterion makes the protocol robust.

5) The Broadcast Tree

Of the multiple tree paths from each switch to the root, at any time only one path will be used to avoid looping of broadcast frames. For this purpose, a switch declares one of its VIDs as Primary VID (PVID). The PVID is decided based hop count in this study. Thus, in this study, switches use the shortest VID from the set of VID's that they have stored, as the PVID. A PVID and the PVID port provide the lowest cost path from a switch to the root.

A switch also records its neighbors who have chosen it as the "PVID parent", noting their PVID as a child-PVID (CPVID) and their port of connection. While a PVID and its port of acquisition connect a switch to the Root, a CPVID port and its port of connection provides the link between a downstream switch and an upstream switch. The PVID, CPVID ports map out the broadcast tree to reach every switch – the broadcast tree is the tree that spans all switches and is used to forward the broadcast frame. We use Figure 2D to explain the broadcast tree defined by MTP. In Figure 4 we show Figure 2D only with the PVID selected by each switch, its port of acquisition and the CPVID port recorded by a switch and the port on which the CPVID was issued. In Figure 4, the connected CPVID and PVID ports using green arrows represent the broadcast tree. Note that the broadcast tree reach is limited to the switches and not extended to the links between the switches. This is in line with the later loop avoidance protocols that do not support hubs or shared media: example IS-IS based protocols. This further simplifies the tree construction as compared to spanning tree protocols.

6) Reducing Failure Detection Time

Failure detection time is one of the major contributors to convergence latency in most routing and loop-avoidance protocols. To reduce failure detection, Bidirectional Failure Detection (BFD) protocols was introduced [13]. BFD can be invoked by any protocol or application that

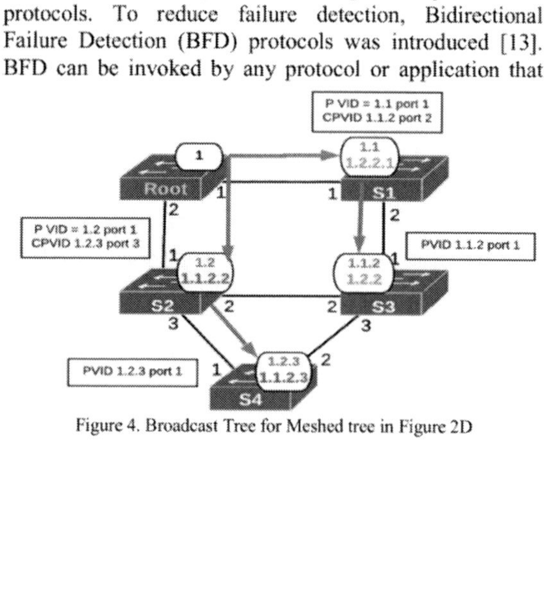

Figure 4. Broadcast Tree for Meshed tree in Figure 2D

requires faster notification on connection failures. It is implemented in the forwarding engine of the system. The idea behind BFD is similar to a 'hello protocol' and it sends hello messages at a higher frequency. However, a flapping interface can generate excessive change notifications in the system resulting in an unstable system. BFD introduces dampening [14] for this purpose, where the client application is not informed if the interface is flapping. *However, during the time that an interface is flapping, frames being forwarded or received via that interface may not be forwarded correctly.*

RSTP did not adopt BFD and instead uses a hello timer of 2 seconds and a dead time interval which is 3 times the hello timer – these are the default settings. This results in a failure detection time of anywhere between 5 to 7 seconds. In the set of studies presented in this article, we used these default settings as they serve as a reference. However, we separately recorded the failure detection time and the protocol recovery time to highlight the significant role played by protocols in the recovery time experienced in networks. It is the protocol recovery time and the messages exchanged during convergence that we compare primarily between RSTP and MTP.

7) Failure Detection with Hysteresis in MTP

The VID based approach in MTP and the storage of multiple VIDs provides a mechanism for us to speed up failure detection with MTP without the need for BFD. This approach also avoids the flapping interface problem. Because there are multiple pre-constructed paths which are identified by the VID's, in the event of a single missing hello message from a neighbor switch, a switch that has a VID derived on the port (of failure) removes this VID immediately into a quarantine table. The switch falls back to the next VID in its VID table. The VID changes (deletes) are advertised in the switched network and other switches if required update their VID table. However, if the port comes up active, this switch will wait for 'n' consecutive hello messages before re-instating the deleted VID from the quarantine table. Maintaining the deleted VID in the quarantine table helps to identify a recovering VID and avoid impacts of interface flapping – we call this the hysteresis approach. The value of 'n' was set to 3 in the studies. This avoids the flapping interface problem and hello messages between switches could be exchanged at a higher frequency. Thus MTP provides an efficient solution to the flapping interface problem.

In this experimental study, we set the hello interval to 1 second and the dead time interval to 2 times the hello interval. The hello interval and dead time interval can be further adjusted to speed up failure detection. The hello messages used in MTP are single byte messages and incur very little overhead- considerably less than BFD messages. Tuning the hello interval and a dead time interval of MTP would be a more desirable approach as there is no need to set up communication between MTP and BFD and also establishing sessions between every pair of switches – which is typically the approach used when BFD is used for failure detection.

With MTP, we are able quarantine the deleted VID and fallback on the next VID as all these VID's are precomputed and stored in the VID table. No re-computation is required on a topology change and MTP bypasses this delay completely. This is the first protocol that can support fast failure detection using a hysteresis approach.

IV. Performance Metrics

The performance metrics analyzed are 1) protocol recovery delay, 2) failure detection delays 3) number of messages exchanged during convergence and the 4) number of port role /states changed (only for RSTP). Metrics 3 and 4 provide a means to assess a protocol's processing needs on topology changes. Typically:

Convergence Delay = Failure Detection Delay + Change Dissemination Delay + Recovery Delay

Dissemination Delay + Recovery Delay = Protocol Recovery Delay.

Protocol Recovery Delay depends on a protocol's recovery process subsequent to failure detection. With RSTP, the protocol recovery latency depends on network size, connectivity, the point of failure on the logical tree i.e. the relative position of the failure point with respect to the root and also on the port role of the failed port. RSTP recovery delay includes dissemination and tree recovery. MTP dissemination and recovery of tree proceed simultaneously. MTP recovery latency has low dependency on the network size/connectivity, the tree pruning is done with minimal number of messages and is significantly faster than RSTP.

A. Protocol Recovery Delay Contributors

In RSTP, in the case of a designated port failure, the switch on the other end of the link connected to the designated port must wait for failure detection before it can send topology change notifications. As per standards specifications, when a designated port fails, the port roles and states stabilize after a handshake between the node whose designated port failed, and any downstream switches connected on other designated ports. Proposal agreements speed up RSTP convergence – but these handshake messages must go down the branch(es) and switches are in 'discarding' state until a concurrence of port role changes arrives from downstream switches. When a root port fails, that switch immediately falls back on the alternate port, if any, else it assumes it is the root switch and messages with its neighbors for a quicker resolution of the tree. Besides, when a root port fails and if there is an alternate port, this port becomes the root port and initiates a TCN. Else it is initiated by a node that receives the changed BPDU from the node with the failed root port. In larger diameter topology this takes time. These are discussed under the protocol evaluation Section.

With MTP, on the deletion of a lost VID, which is immediate on failure detection, a delete message is sent out on all control ports of this switch (i.e. ports connecting to other switches running MTP). The switches that receive the delete message, remove any VIDs derived from the deleted VID and further propagate the message. Frame forwarding is impacted, only if the PVID in a switch is deleted. This can be noted in the results that we recorded during the prototype evaluations.

Using Figure 5, we explain the tree pruning process with MTP, on topology changes. In Figure 5, the link between the root switch and switch S1 is failed at port 1 of switch S1. On the failure of interface (port) 1, switch S1 deletes VID 1.1 acquired on port 1. It then sends out a delete message on its port 2 (containing the deleted VID 1.1). Switch S3 deletes its primary VID 1.1.2, moves its VID 1.2.1.2 as its PVID and sends out a delete message on its ports 2 and 3. Switch S2 deletes VID 1.1.2.2 that is derived from 1.1.2, but this has no change on the PVID. Similarly switch S4 deletes VID 1.12.3. Note the change in the broadcast tree (indicated with green arrows in Figure 5) –was achieved with three messages, as seen in Figure 5.

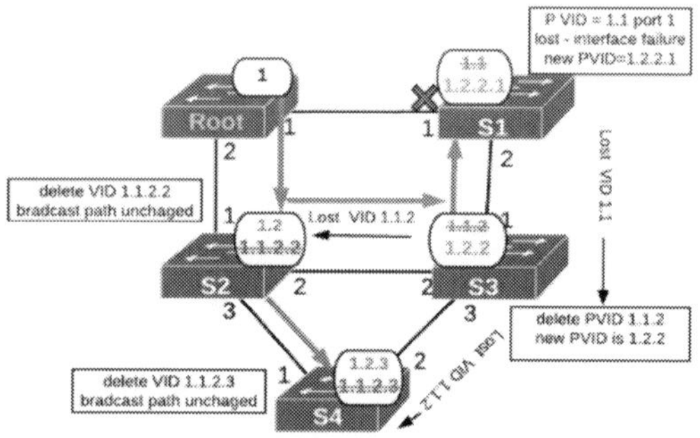

Figure 5. Meshed Tree Pruning on Link Root-B1 Failure

There is only one PVID change – thus, disruption to the broadcast tree is minimal and tree convergence is very fast.

V. PROTOTYPE EVALUATIONS

The hardware for the implementation of MTP was acquired using GENI testbeds [10]. GENI is an open infrastructure for at scale networking and distributed systems research and education that spans the United States. It provides the infrastructure needed to carry out networking research. A set of compute resources like switches and network links to connect them can be acquired from GENI to set up the desired topology. RSTP is available on Open View switches at certain GENI sites and has been used in this performance study. MTP code was written in the C language and tested and deployed on GENI switches. The computer resources used from GENI ran Linux distributions. We used the Linux kernel networking stack to create raw Ethernet frames to carry MTP messages. The type field in the Ethernet frame was set to an unused number and messages sent by MTP would be picked up at Layer 2 and delivered to MTP processes at a receiving switch.

Identical topologies were used to evaluate the two protocols. To emulate identical operational conditions, we biased a switch's priority in networks running RSTP so it would get elected the root. An identical positioned switch in networks running MTP, was designated as the root switch. We used three different sized topologies: a simple 5-node 2-loop topology, a moderate 8-node 4-loop topology, and a more connected 17-node topology, with 7-hop diameter – the max specified in IEEE 802.1 standards [2]. This allowed us to assess and understand the protocol operation in a simple topology and study how the protocol scaled with increased network size and in more connected topologies.

A. Methodology

Tshark [11] was installed at all active GENI node interfaces to capture RSTP Bridge Protocol Data Units (BPDUs). RSTP operational states were logged at every node. The logs and captures were scanned to collect BPDUs generated and port roles/state changes as RSTP converged on topology changes. Chrony [12] was installed in all nodes to ensure the clocks on the nodes were consistent and time drifts minimal. GENI allows recording timestamps to an accuracy of 1 millisecond (ms). MTP code recorded events using the system's timer, with a timing accuracy of microseconds. Automation scripts were written in Python, to

- upload and execute the code in the GENI nodes,
- continuously collect the results into log files as the protocol is running at the GENI nodes,
- transfer the log files into our local system, and scan the log files to collect relevant data,

The automation scripts were written to repeat the experiment in each topology 5 times. The averages of these 5 runs were then recorded in the tables provided below.

B. Small Topology (5 switches)

In tests running RSTP, the *Convergence Time* (CT) is the time when a port is brought down to the time when ports that are changing roles and states in all switches settle down to their final roles and states. The *Failure Detection Time* (FDT is the time a switch across from the failed port recognized the failure and initiates action. The *Protocol Recovery Time* (PRT) is the time taken by the protocol to recover from the failure and converge after failure detection. Thus, CT is FDT plus PRT. In certain cases, we noticed that Topology Change Notifications (TCN) continue even after the port roles and states (PRS) stabilized. This is because, switches are required to send TCNs for a duration of tcWhile [8]. This was discounted in the calculations.

The RSTP 5-node topology with port roles (R for Root

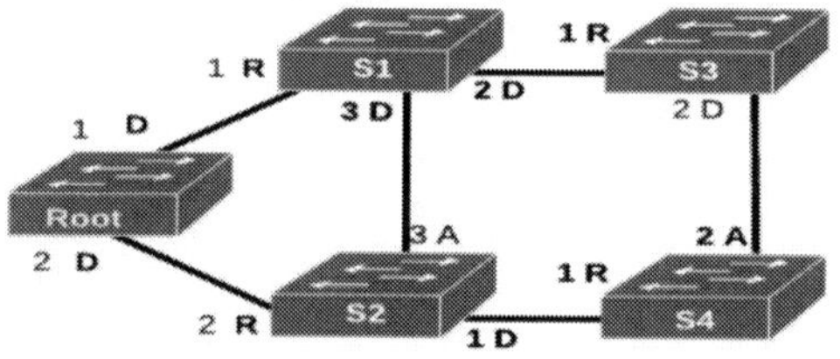

Figure 6. RSTP 5 Node Topology with Port Roles

port, D for Designated port and A for Alternate port) are shown in Figure 6. The performance recorded in Table 1 reflect the dependencies on the port roles of ports that were failed noted in column 2 from Table 1. For the 5-node topology the test cases are noted in column 1 from Table 1. Single link failures were introduced by disabling a port in a switch. S1(1) indicates failed port 1 in switch S1. The role of the disabled port is noted in column 2 - D for Designated port and R for Root. PRS changes and TCN message exchanges that happen during convergence are noted. Under the FDT column we also note the switch that initiated change notifications.

1) Convergence Process in 5-node RSTP Topology

Root Port Failures: This happens in cases 2, 5, 7. Note that there is no FDT time, as the switch with the failed port initiates TCNs immediately. However, in case 2 the PRT was recorded as 3.523 seconds with 13 port role and state changes, (which indicates message exchanges such as proposal-agreements among switches) and 20 TCNs. In case 5, the PRT was recorded as 18 ms, with 5 port role/state changes and 26 TCNs. Under case 7, the PRT is very low, as this required S4 to fallback on its alternate port. The failure was at the edge of the tree – and this did not require TCN dissemination.

Designated Port Failures: Cases 1, 3, 4, and 6 relate to designated port failures. In all these cases the PRT was recorded to be around 3 seconds and TCNs varied from 20 to 30 messages. In certain cases the PRS were as low as 3 while we recorded 9 PRS under case 1.

2) Convergence in 5-switch MTP Topology

The broadcast tree established by MTP is given by the PVID and CPVID ports as discussed using Figure 4. In Figure 7, the PVID and CPVID ports are shown for the 5-node topology. Ports identical to the ones failed in the RSTP topology were failed in the MTP network. With MTP, in certain cases (e.g. 3 and 5 in Table 2), failing a port has no impact on the broadcast tree. *This is because the MTP broadcast tree stops at the switches and is not extended to links.*

TABLE I. RSTP CONVERGENCE IN A 5-NODE TOPOLOGY

Case	Failed Port - Role	FDT-initiated	PRT	PRS	TCNs
1	Root(2) ---D	5.115s by S2	**3.519s**	9	24
2	S1(1) -----R	0s by S1	**3.523s**	13	20
3	S1(3) -----D	4.030s by S2	**2.999s**	3	16
4	S1(2)------D	4.810s by S3	**3.018s**	8	25
5	S3(1) ----R	0s by S3	**18ms**	5	26
6	S3(2)------D	4.733s by S4	**3.164s**	3	18
7	S4(1) -----R	0s by S4	**9ms**	5	0
R- Root port, D- Designated port, FDT – Failure Detection time, PRT – Protocol Recovery Time, CT- Convergence time, PRS – Port/Role State Changes, TCN – Topology Change Notifications					

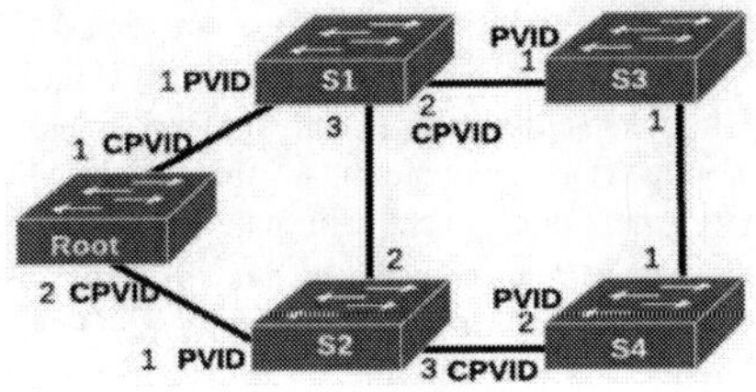

Figure 7. MTP 5 Node Topology with PVID, CPVID

TABLE II. MTP CONVERGENCE IN A 5-NODE TOPOLOGY

Case	Failed Port – (C)PVID	FDT	PRT	Messages
1	Root(1)-----CPVID	1.15s	**1.5 ms**	2
2	S1(1)-----PVID	2.71s	**0.14 ms**	3
3	S1(3)-----X	No Impact		
4	S1(2)-----CPVID		**1.8 ms**	4
5	S3(1)----- X	No Impact		
6	S3(2)-----PVID		**1.77 ms**	2
7	S4(1)----- PVID		**0.7 ms**	2
X – Port not part of tree				

PVID Port Failures: Case 2, 6 and 7 involve a PVID port failure. In each of the cases the number of messages required to prune the tree is less than 3 – which should be compared to the number of TCN messages exchanged with RSTP. Following the messages exchanged, in case 2, switch S1 informs switches S2 and S3 about the failed VID, Switch S2 updates its PVID and informs its new PVID parent. The PRT is 1ms or less in these cases which should be compared to approximately 3 sec PRT recorded with RSTP.

CPVID Port Failures: In cases 1 and 4, the CPVID port is failed. The PRT with MTP is around 1.5 ms several magnitudes less than a similar port failure with RSTP. This value is less than the lowest recorded with RSTP (under case 7, when a port at the tree edge was failed). In most cases with MTP the tree resolves with less than 5 MTP messages.

3) Summary 5-switch Protocol recovery

The profound difference in PRT noticed between RSTP and MTP is because of the VIDs used by MTP to simplify both tree construction and pruning operations. With MTP, the VIDs maintain the tree information, whereas with RSTP, each switch has to maintain its ports in Root, Designated or Alternate role to define the spanning tree. Thus, in the event of a topology changes, all switches exchange BPDUs, to resolve the port roles and repair the tree.

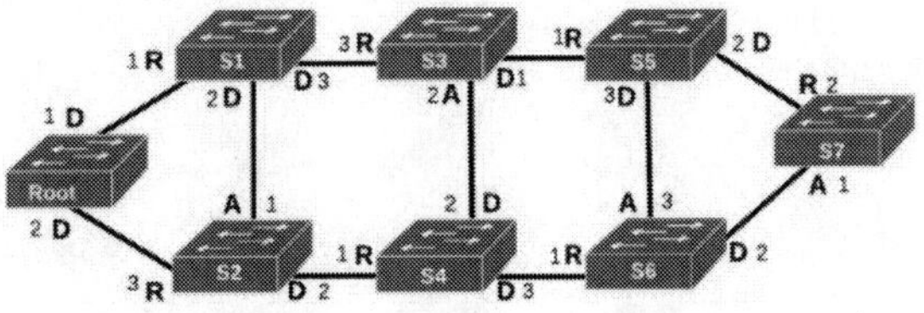

Figure 8. RSTP 8 Node Topology with Port Roles

C. Medium Topology (8 switches)

The 8-switch topology running RSTP, along with the port roles is given in Figure 8. As before we failed single ports as indicated in column 2 of Table 3. We also record the port roles.

1) Convergence in 8-node RSTP Topology

Root Port Failures: Cases 2, 5, 8, and 11 record data on Root port failures. Notice that the FDT is 0 seconds as the switch with the failed Root port initiates TCN immediately on the port failure detection. However, the PRT is approximately 3 seconds except in the case 11, where the failed Root port was at the tree edge, and the switch had an alternate port, which took over immediately on the root port failure. Compared to the PRS and TCNs recorded for the 5-switch topology, in this case there is an increase in the PRS and TCNs. This is because these messages are generated by more switches, and more switches change their port roles/states. This could contribute to high PRT. This also indicates instability in the network while the network is stabilizing after the port failure.

In case 2, on *S1(1)* (root port) failure, S1 immediately initiates recovery. However, as S1 does not have an alternate port, S1 assumes it is the root and negotiates with its neighbors. Hence the PRT was 3.032s. Failure of S5(1) (root port) in the middle of the network resulted in a PRT of 3.525s, even though S5 immediately takes action on its port failure. Failure of S7(2), (root port) edge of the tree, resulted in its alternate port taking over within 12ms.

Designated Port Failures: Cases 1, 3, 4, 6, 7, 9, and 10 record data collected on a Designated port failure. The PRT is again approximately 3 seconds. In case 3, even though there were only 3 PRS, a total of 37 TCNs were recorded and RSTP still took approximately 3 seconds of PRT.

The PRT with RSTP is very much dependent on the point of failure with respect to the root and also if the failed port was designated or root.

2) Convergence in 8-Node MTP Topology

The 8-switch MTP topology is given Figure 9. Instead of providing the broadcast tree, we decided to show the three VIDs stored at each switch. The PVIDs at each switch connected by red lines and show the broadcast tree. Following the VID dotted decimal format the multiple paths from each switch to the root switch will be clear. The green lines and purple lines show how the other 2 VIDs were derived at each switch. They also show how the VIDs provide the path from a non-root switch to the root switch. In Table 4, we record only 9 cases as we did not record port failures that had no impact on the broadcast tree. PRT is still very low – tens of ms. In certain cases we recorded microseconds and these are noted as <1ms in the table.

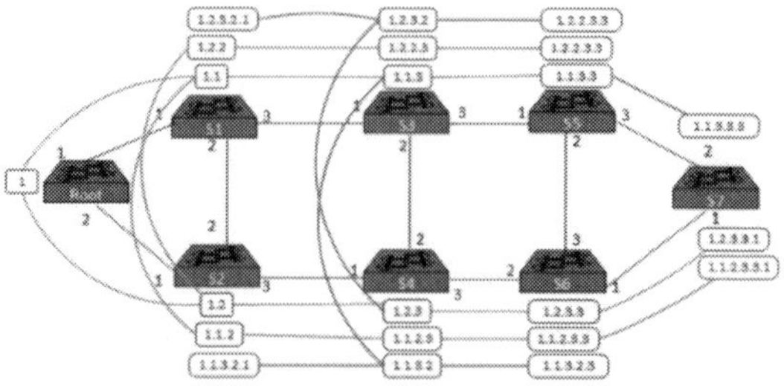

Figure 9. MTP 8 -Node Topology with Meshed

TABLE III. RSTP CONVERGENCE IN A 8-NODE TOPOLOGY

Case	Failed Port --Role	FDT-initiated	PRT	PRS	TCN
1	Root(1) -----D	5.037s by S1	**3.021s**	22	75
2	S1(1)-----R	0s S1	**3.032s**	19	68
3	S1(2) -----D	4.023s by S2	**3.005s**	3	37
4	S1(3)-----D	5.206s by S3	**3.027s**	13	59
5	S4(1)-----R	0s S4	**2.528s**	15	72
6	S4(2)-----D	5.017s by S4	**3.004s**	3	37
7	S4(3)-----D	5.526s by S6	**3.014s**	6	30
8	S5(1)----R	0s S5	**3.525s**	15	40
9	S5(2)-----D	4.199s by S7	**3.012s**	6	35
10	S5(3)-----D	5.018s by S6	**3.005s**	3	39
11	S7(2)-----R	0s S7	**12 ms**	3	36

PVID Port Failures: Cases 2, 5, 8 and 11 are PVID port failures – i.e. the main path between that switch and root switch failed. This is however repaired by MTP in around17 ms, when the PVID at a switch closer to the root failed (worst case). As the PVID port is further away from the switch the recovery time with MTP drops down – and is less than 1 ms in cases 11 and 8. The fast recovery is attributed to the fact that the only action in these cases is reinstating the next VID in the VID table as the PVID. Note the very low number of message exchanges.

TABLE IV. MTP CONVERGENCE IN A 8-NODE TOPOLOGY

Case	Failed Port– (C)PVID	FDT	PRT	Messages
1	Root(1)-----CPVID	1.740s	**14.6ms**	6
2	S1(1)-----PVID		**17ms**	4
3	S1(2)	No Impact		
4	S1(3)-----CPVID	1.024s	**15ms**	5
5	S4(1)-----PVID		**6ms**	4
6	S4(2)	No Impact		
7	S4(3)-----CPVID	2.407s	**7ms**	4
8	S5(1)-----PVID	2.290s	**< 1ms**	4
9	S5(2)	No Impact		
10	S5(3)-----CPVID	1.046s	**5ms**	3
11	S7(2)-----PVID	2.756s	**< 1ms**	0

CPVID Port Failure: In cases 1, 4, 7 and 10 a CPVID port was failed. The PRT in these cases also reduced as the failure port was further away from the Root. Closer to the root the PRT was around 15ms, further from the root the PRT was around 5 to 6 ms. The low number of message exchanges are primarily the delete messages sent to prune the VIDs from the deleted VID – as described in Section IV.A, Figure 5.

D. Large Topology (17 switches)

Figure 10 shows a bigger, and more connected 17-node topology, with a diameter of 7 hops. A higher diameter topology should result in higher convergence times, but the higher connectivity counteracts this. With higher connectivity, there are several alternate ports at switches S4, S6, S7, S9, S10, S11, S14 and S15. In Figure 10, we also show the spanning tree constructed by RSTP. We will refer to this tree when comparing results from the MTP 17-node topology. The single port failures are noted in column 1 Table 5.

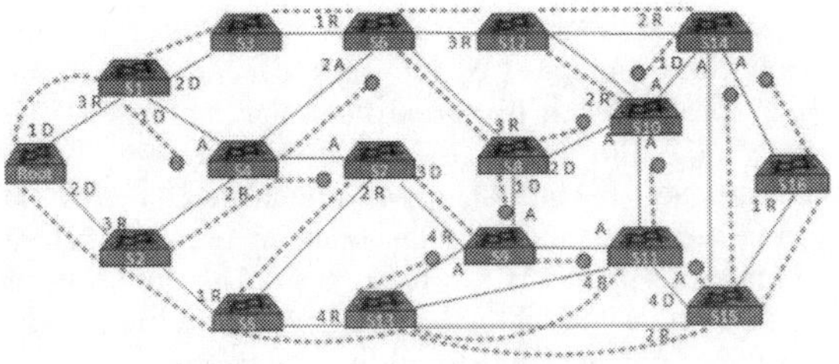

Figure 10. RSTP 17- Node Topology with Port Roles and Broadcast Tree

1) Convergence in 17-Node RSTP Topology

Root Port Failures: Cases 4, 5, 9, 11, 12 and 14 introduce Root port failures. Except for case 12 in all other cases the PRT is low and varies from 15 ms to 40 ms. In case 12, the PRT is around 3 seconds –the reason is that at switch S15, there are no alternat ports to take over immediately. Though this is at the farther end from the Root, the switch declares itself as root switch which then takes time to resolve. In all other cases, the switch with a failed root port had an alternate port. The number of TCN messages exchanged are very high.

Designated Port Failures: All other failure cases were designated port failures and the PRT averaged around 3 seconds.

2) Convergence in 17-node MTP Topology

Figure 11 shows the 17-node MTP topology, with Broadcast Tree supported by PVIDs and CPVIDs.

PVID Port Failures: They are cases 4, 7, 9, 10, 12 and 14. In all these cases the PRT varies from 12 ms to 6 ms. The convergence is achieved with very few message exchanges much lower than RSTP.

CPVID Port Failures: These are cases 1, 3, and 13. The maximum PRT recorded was for case 1, where the failure of a port at the root switch results in the tree originating from this VID which had to be pruned through 9 messages. For cases 3 and 13 it was as low as 5 and 3 ms. *Compared to RSTP – where every change resulted in transients, this indicates a major reduction in processing overhead. PRT is in tens of ms compared to RSTP.*

TABLE V. RSTP CONVERGENCE IN A 17-NODE TOPOLOGY

Case	Failed Port - Role	FDT	PRT	PRS	TCN
1	Root (1)-----D	4.501s by S3	3.462s	26	100
2	S1 (1)-----D	5.024s by S4	3.010s	3	80
3	S1 (2)-----D	4.086s by S3	3.028s	10	80
4	S1 (3)-----R	0s by S1	***40ms***	20	110
5	S7 (2)-----R	0s by S7	***24ms***	3	90
6	S7 (3)-----D	4.680s by S9	3.019s	6	85
7	S8 (1)-----D	3.231s by S8	3.000s	3	84
8	S8 (2)-----D	3.998s by S10	3.001s	3	84
9	S8 (3)-----R	0s by S8	***32ms***	10	106
10	S14 (1)-----D	4.466s by S10	3.007s	3	93
11	S14 (2)-----R	0s by S14	***25 ms***	3	100
12	S15 (2)-----R	0s by S15	3.054s	30	153
13	S15 (4)----D	5.475s by S11	3.011s	3	80
14	S16 (1)-----R	0s by S16	***15ms***	5	88

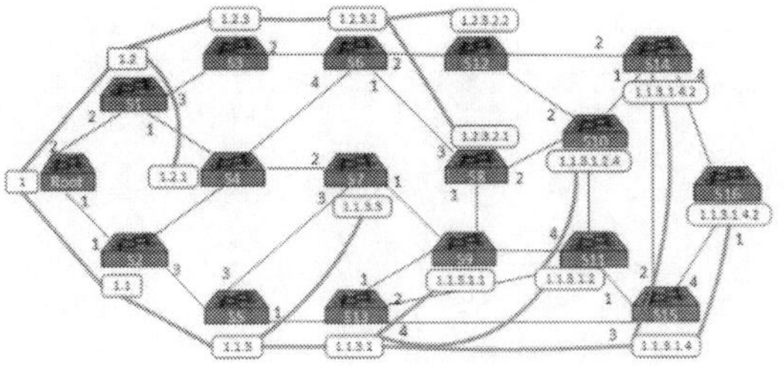

Figure 11. MTP 17- Node Topology with Broadcast Tree

VI. SUMMARY

MTP and RSTP were evaluated for several failure test cases where we tracked the number of message exchanges and port role/state changes (for RSTP). The high number of message exchanges with RSTP indicate the complexity of the convergence process which in turn is reflected in the convergence latency. To capture the significant difference in PRT and messages exchanged we plotted MTP vs RSTP data on a log scale. They are provided in Figures 12-15. Figures 12 and 13 capture the PRT experienced for single port failures in the 5 and 8 node topologies. We used a log scale for the latency (seconds) to highlight the difference in PRT with MTP and RSTP. The green line in the figures show the cases where the port failure had no impact on broadcast tree. In certain root port failures RSTP recovered fast if there existed an alternate port. MTP consistently had a PRT lower than these cases of RSTP. The no impact points further prove the improved network stability with MTP for single port failures.

In Figures 14 and 15, we plotted the number of messages exchanged on a topology change for MTP vs RSTP. While RSTP exchanged 10 to 100 messages, MTP exchanged less than 10 messages. This shows how lightweight MTP is as compared to RSTP. Even when the PRT was low, RSTP still exchanged several messages, the overhead and operational complexity with RSTP is very much higher than MTP.

TABLE VI. MTP CONVERGENCE IN A 17-NODE TOPOLOGY

Case	Failed Port – (C)PVID	FDT	PRT	Messages
1	Root (1)-----CPVID	2.763s by S2	**36ms**	9
2	S 1 (1)	No Impact		
3	S 1 (3)-----CPVID	2.726s by S3	**5ms**	2
4	S1 (2)-----PVID	-	**11ms**	4
5	S7 (1)	No Impact		
6	S7 (2)	No Impact		
7	S7 (3)-----PVID		**5.4ms**	2
8	S8 (2)	No Impact		
9	S8 (3)-----PVID	2.450 by S6	**7ms**	3
10	S14 (2)-----PVID	1.911 by S12	**6ms**	2
11	S14 (4)	No Impact		
12	S15 (3)-----PVID		**12ms**	5
13	S15 (4)-----CPVID	2.453s by S16	**3ms**	2
14	S16 (1)-----PVID	2.946s by S15	**6ms**	1

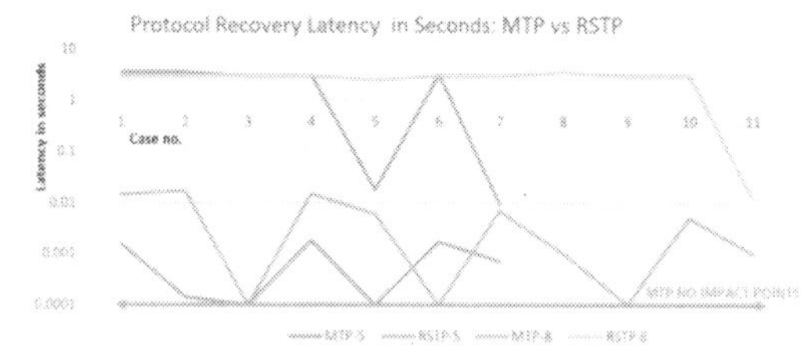

Figure 12. PRT - MTP vs RSTP (5 and 8 switches)

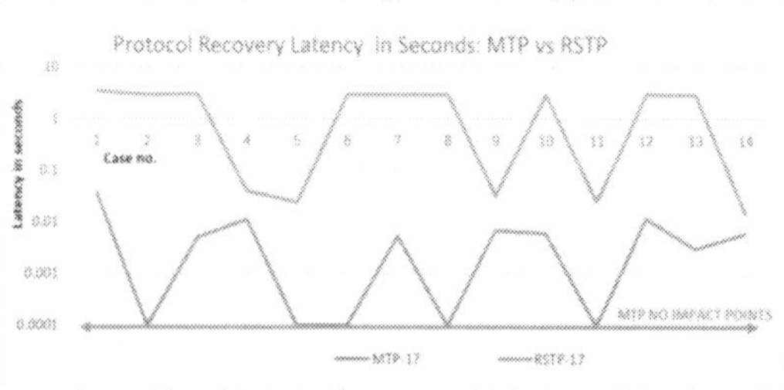

Figure 13. Message Exchanges MTP vs RSTP (5 and 8 switches)

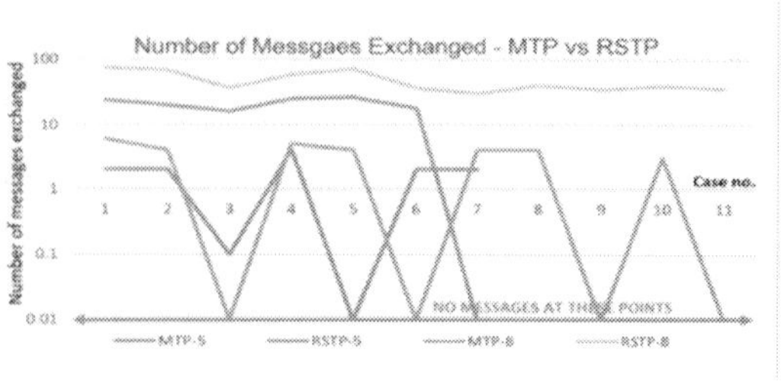

Figure 14. PRT - MTP vs RSTP (5 and 8 switch topology)

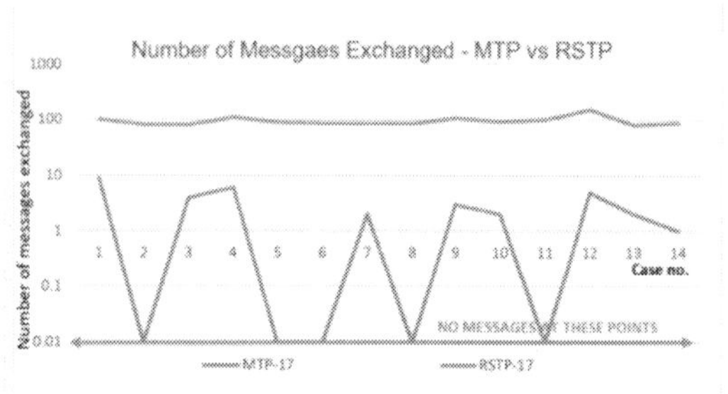

Figure 15. Message Exchange MTP vs RSTP (17 switch topology)

VII. CONCLUSION

MTP uses a novel meshed tree algorithm to construct and stores multiple tree information constructed from a single root, which is carried in simple structured VIDs. The VID information is very powerful both for tree construction, maintenance and pruning on failures. The presented data and tree construction and maintenance information indicates the robustness of the protocol and high resiliency to failures offered by MTP. Using MTP in customer, SP and BP networks will outperform RSTP and IS-IS based solutions in all aspects – performance, resource usage and reduced operational complexity. In this article, we limit the comparison to RSTP. Future work will extend the comparison studies to IS-IS based solutions.

REFERENCES

[1] P. Willis and N. Shenoy, "A Meshed Tree Protocol for Loop Avoidance in Switched Networks", Workshop, IEEE International Conference on Computing, Networking and Communications, 18-21 Feb. 2019, Honoulu, Hawai, USA, ICNC 2019

[2] IEEE 802.1w - Rapid Reconfiguration of Spanning Tree, supplement to ISO/IEC 15802-3:1998 (IEEE Std 802.1D-1998)

[3] R. Perlman, "Rbridges: Transparent Routing", IEEE Proceedings of Infocomm 2004.

[4] R. Perlman, D. Eastlake, G. D. Dutt and A. G. Gai, "Rbridges: Base Protocol Specification", RFC 6325, July 2011.

[5] J. Touch, R. Perlman, "Transparent Interconnection of Lots of Links (TRILL): Problem and Applicability Statement", RFC 5556.

[6] P. Ashwood-Smith (24 February 2011). "Shortest Path Bridging IEEE 802.1aq Overview". Huawei. Retrieved 11 May 2012.

[7] "IS-IS Extensions Supporting IEEE 802.1aq Shortest Path Bridging", http://tools.ietf.org/html/rfc6329. IETF. April 2012. Retrieved 2 April 2012. Retrieved 4th Nov 2014.

[8] IEEE LAN/MAN Standards Committee of the IEEE Computer Society, ed. (1998). ANSI/IEEE Std 802.1D, 1998 Edition, Part 3: Media Access Control (MAC) Bridges

[9] L. Goodman, A. Lauschke, and E. W. Weisstein, "Dijkstra's Algorithm," MathWorld—AWolfram Web Resource. [Online]. Available: https://mathworld.wolfram.com/DijkstrasAlgorithm.html. [Accessed: 10-Jun-2020].

[10] www.geni.net [Accessed: 10-Jun-2020].

[11] https://www.wireshark.org/docs/man-pages/tshark.html, Retrieved 31 Oct. 2018

[12] https://chrony.tuxfamily.org/ [Accessed:31-July-2020]

[13] Bidirectional Forwarding Detection https://tools.ietf.org/html/rfc5880#section-3.1 [Accessed:1-May-2020]

[14] BFD Dampening https://www.cisco.com/c/en/us/td/docs/ios-xml/ios/iproute_bfd/configuration/xe-3s/irb-xe-3s-book/irb-bfd-damp.html [Accessed:31-July-2020]

An Authentication Technique to Handle DDoS Attacks in Proxy-Based Architecture

Poonam Dharam
Computer Science and Information Systems
Saginaw Valley State University
Saginaw, MI, USA
email: pdharam@svsu.edu

Jarin Musarrat
Computer Science and Information Systems
Saginaw Valley State University
Saginaw, MI, USA
email: jmusarra@svsu.edu

Abstract— **Recent years have witnessed an increase in Distributed Denial of Service (DDoS) attacks that overwhelm available network and backend server resources such as bandwidth, buffers, etc. To handle such attacks, proxy-based network architectures have been implemented to manage and Load Balance incoming traffic by spawning new servers in the event of unexpected rise in network traffic. However, DDoS attacks continue to persist with the attack target shifting from the main backend application servers to proxy servers. The redirection of users to one of the available proxy servers results in the discovery of their (proxy server's) IP address. A botnet can then be used by the attacker to generate a huge amount of traffic and direct it to the proxy server, thus causing DDoS. In this paper, we propose an authentication technique to ensure the uniform distribution of the incoming requests and to avoid/drop the illegitimate requests from occupying servers' resources. Our simulation results show that the proposed solution detects and handles DDoS attacks in an efficient manner.**

Keywords-Distributed Denial of Service; proxy-based architecture; flooding attacks.

I. INTRODUCTION

Internet Distributed Denial of Service (DDoS) attacks have emerged as one of the biggest threats to Internet security, with thousands of them occurring every year. Hackers are turning to DDoS to bring down organizations' services and to compromise their sensitive data. Recent times have witnessed a dramatic increase in such attacks due to the declining cost of launching an attack and the popularity of Internet of Things (IoT) devices [1] that could be used as botnets. Recently, the Mirai botnet [2], that brought down major services including Twitter, Netflix, CNN (Cable News Network), and many others, was largely made up of IoT devices such as digital cameras and Digital Video Recorder (DVR) players [3].

The DDoS attack mainly targets the availability of a service by exhausting the resources associated with the service. In the context of computer and communications, the focus is generally on network services that are attacked over their network connection. A classic flooding DDoS attack [4] involves a significant amount of malicious traffic directed towards a target server. The volume of the attack traffic can be scaled up by using multiple systems that are either compromised user workstations, PCs, or IoT. For example, attackers identify devices that use default login credentials to gain backdoor access to them and install an attack agent that they can control. A large collection of such systems under the control of one attacker can be created, collectively forming a botnet. This traffic overwhelms any legitimate traffic, effectively denying legitimate users' access to the server.

Internet Control Message Protocol (ICMP), User Datagram Protocol (UDP), or Transmission Control Protocol (TCP) SYN packets are most commonly used for flooding attacks. Any packet that is permitted to flow over the links, towards the targeted system, can be used to fill up the available capacity. Such attacks flood the network link with a huge number of malicious packets in turn competing with regular user traffic flowing to the server. Many packets, mostly valid traffic, will be dropped on the path to the server due to the congestion caused by flooding. For example, a DDoS flooding attack on a Web Server involves several valid Hyper Text Transport Protocol (HTTP) requests, each using significant server resources. This then limits the server's ability to service requests from other users. For instance, HTTP requests use TCP as transport layer protocol. For each TCP connection made, some amount of buffer space at the server's end is reserved for reliable data transfer, congestion control, and flow control. Also, the server only has a limited amount of memory for user buffer space. Once the TCP connections fill up the server's buffer, future requests will be either cached or dropped until the buffer space frees up [5]. Another example would be a Web Server that includes the ability to make database queries. If a database query that takes a large amount of time for the server to respond can be constructed, then an attacker could generate many such queries to overload the server. This limits the ability to respond to valid requests from other servers.

Most of the DDoS attacks use forged source addresses to generate large volumes of packets with the target system as destination and randomly selected, usually different, source address for each packet. This, in turn, makes it harder to identify the attacking system. Also, the volume of network traffic can be easily scaled up by using multiple systems.

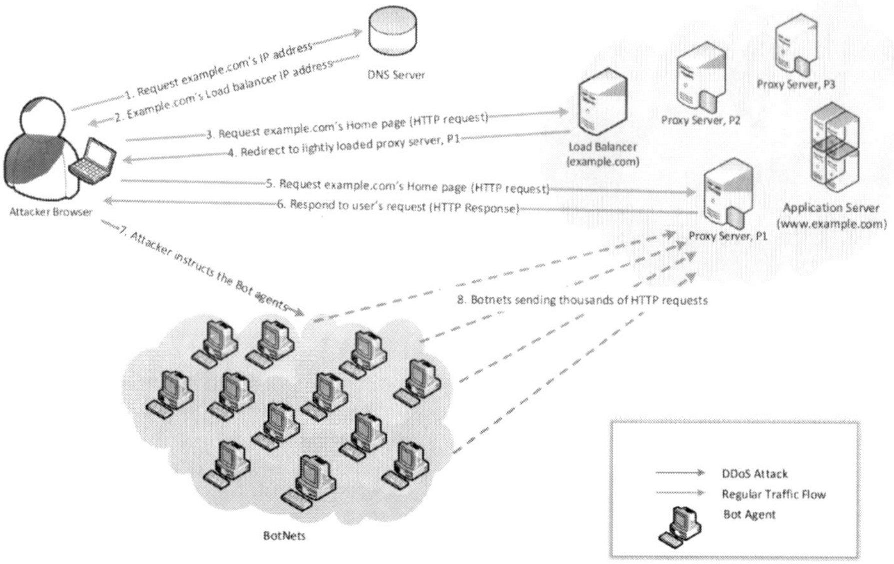

Figure 1. Example of a DDoS attack in proxy-based architecture.

In order to handle such attacks, proxy-based network architectures [6] have been implemented to manage and load-balance incoming traffic by spawning new servers in the event of unexpected rise in network traffic. Proxy-based architectures usually have multiple layers of redirection between the user and the application servers. A Load Balancer (LB) placed between the proxy server [7] and the backend server redirects incoming users to one of the available, lightly loaded proxy servers. Proxy servers hold a copy of the content present in the original servers and process the incoming user request on behalf of the original application server. A proxy server communicates with the original server in the event of missing or outdated information. Also, in case of unexpected rise in incoming traffic, cloud services are used to spawn additional proxy servers to handle the traffic. Thus, organizations do not have to invest a lot for in house proxy servers, but instead pay for the duration of usage. With such an architecture, the attack surface has shifted to proxy servers and DDoS attacks continue to exist.

To understand the limitations of using a proxy-based architecture in handling DDoS attacks, consider a Web service provided by a combination of proxy servers and a backend application server, as shown in Figure 1. Also, consider a client trying to access a Web page www.example.com. We now list the sequence of steps that take place:

1. The client types in the URL in the browser
2. The browser resolves the domain name by talking to the Domain Name Server (DNS) and getting an equivalent IP address (that actually corresponds to the Load Balancer's IP address)
3. Next, the browser sends an HTTP request to the LB which then finds a proxy server that is lightly loaded
4. The LB then redirects the user to the assigned proxy server
5. The client then directly talks to the proxy server.

The LB redirects the session to one of the active proxies at random. LB-to-proxy redirection by domain name requires that clients obtain proxy details (IP, port number) by DNS and then contact their proxies directly. Through this process, the attacker learns the IP address of an active proxy. Once the IP address of the proxy server is learnt, a DDoS attack can be launched by the botnets by generating a huge number of packets with the proxy server's IP address as the destination [8].

One of the main reasons for such attacks to happen is due to the attackers being aware of the identity of the application servers (IP address and port numbers) hosting the application – the LB-to-proxy redirection by domain name where the client gets the IP address of the proxy server and is on its own in communicating with the server. Once the IP address of a proxy server is known, the attacker can directly launch an attack using a botnet on that proxy server. To handle this problem, we need to ensure that every user directed to a proxy is done so by the Load Balancer. Thus, we can guarantee that the LB is aware of the number of users per proxy. In such cases, any user request directed to a proxy without contacting an LB would be a possible attacker traffic

The rest of our paper is organized as follows. Related work is discussed in Section II. Our proposed solution is described in Section III followed by the experimental setup and results in Section IV. Future work and Conclusions are discussed in Sections V and VI, respectively.

II. RELATED WORK

Most of the existing solutions in this area focus on (a) Moving Target Defense (MTD), and (b) extending the available resources to support increased user requirements. MTD provides a dynamic environment to periodically shift or change the attack surface thus introducing uncertainty for the attackers, thereby hindering their ability to plan effective attacks.

In [9], Venkatesan et al. identify an attack pattern called proxy-harvesting attack which enables malicious clients to collect information about a large number of proxies before launching a DDoS attack. To mitigate ongoing attacks due to proxy-harvesting attack, the authors propose a static client-to-proxy assignment strategy to isolate compromised clients, thereby reducing the impact of attacks. Each client has a binding to a particular server, which persists even if the client logs outs and logs back in. The main challenge with such a strategy is the overhead of maintaining the assignment/ state information and mapping it every time a user request comes in.

In [10], Jia et al. use cloud platforms to host proxies. Incoming requests are validated by a lookup server and the authorized users are directed to one of the existing proxies. In case of an unexpected rise in traffic targeting them, instances of proxies are created in the cloud, for a short period of time, and the existing users associated with the attacked proxies are distributed among the newly spawned proxies. Random shuffling of users is done before assigning them to the new proxies, thus trying to weed out the illegitimate/attacker's traffic.

Another Web protection service is Moving Target Defense Against Internet Denial of Service Attacks (MOTAG) designed by Wang *et al.* [11], which works by hiding the application server location behind the proxy servers. MOTAG is based on a cloud environment where it decreases the availability of resources to limit the impact of an attack. However, there are down points in MOTAG as it does not handle the situation of overhead associated with instantiating and maintaining new proxies.

In Wood et al. [12], the authors proposed Denial of Service Elusion (DoSE), a cloud-based architecture. In DoSE, each client is associated with a risk value that estimates the chances of a client getting a DoS attack. Each proxy is then defined with an upper bound that it can handle. During the attack, the DoSE redirects the client to proxy servers based on the risk calculation. This is similar to MOTAG, and by maintaining a stage for each client, DoSE limits the proxy numbers used to identify insiders.

In MOVE [13], a subset of network elements and target services accept traffic from a subset of overlay nodes. Once the DDoS attack is mitigated, the target service is moved to a new host. However, in order to make this mechanism work, the solution has to rely a lot on large-scale adoption and network elements. This limits the defense approach that underlies behind the targeted servers.

In spite of the existence of various mitigation techniques, DDoS attacks in proxy-based architecture still continue to exist. One of the main reasons is the overhead involved in either migrating the existing clients or spawning additional resources to handle additional traffic. To overcome the identified challenges, in this paper, we design a client-to-proxy assignment and authentication scheme that finds a lightly loaded proxy and returns the IP address along with the unique ID to the client. The client then talks to the proxy server by exchanging its unique ID. Only the user with a valid ID is allowed to communicate with the proxy. We thus make sure that every user directed to a proxy is authenticated by the LB.

III. PROPOSED SOLUTION

In this section, we present a unique tag technique that can be used to authenticate if a client is directed by a LB or not.

The DDoS attack exploits the LB-to-proxy redirection scheme i.e., when a client request arrives at the Load Balancer, it returns the IP address of a lightly loaded proxy server P_i to the client. The client then initiates a TCP connection directly with the proxy server P_i. An insider client is an attacker who manages to bypass the authentication system and connect to the proxy server. Once the insider gets some information related to a proxy server such as IP address and port number, the insider in turn shares that information with an external botnet. Thus, an insider client, aware of the IP address of the proxy server, can in turn initiate/launch a DDoS attack targeting the proxy server by directing the attack traffic from distributed bots towards the proxy server's IP address.

One of the possible ways to handle the above discussed attack scenario is ensuring that each client, requesting a TCP connection with an available proxy server, is directed by the Load Balancer.

Let us consider a simple example where Bob wants to request a Web page from www.example.com and, hence, types in the URL in his browser, as shown in Figure 2.

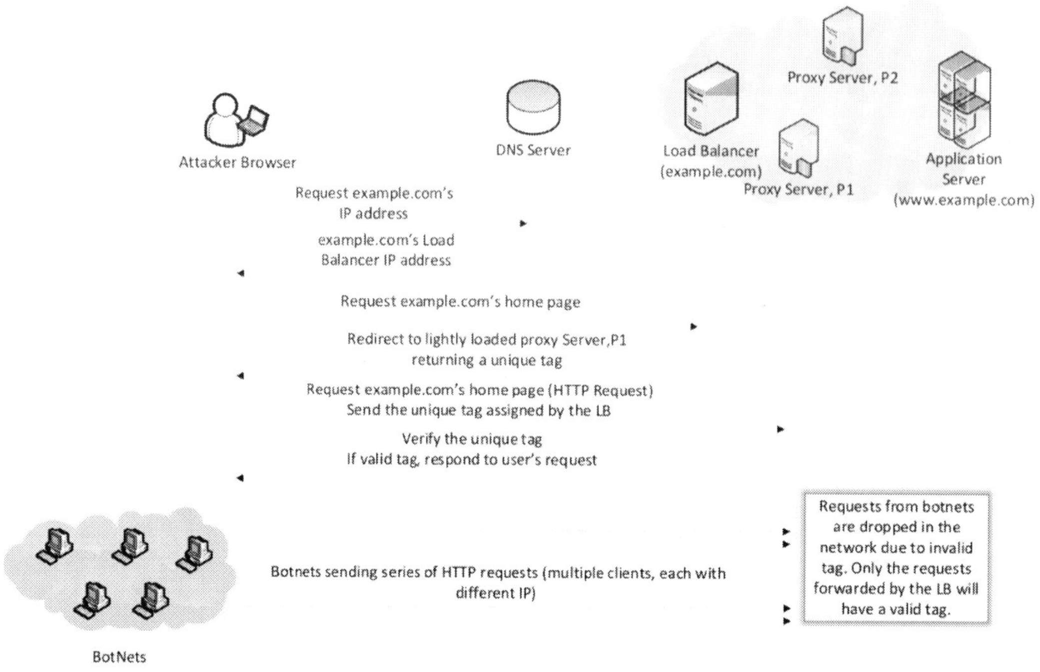

Figure 2. Our proposed solution.

We now list the sequence of steps that takes place:

1. Bob's browser talks to the DNS server requesting for example.com's IP address; DNS returns the IP address corresponding to the LB;

2. Bob's browser then sends a HTTP request to the LB, requesting to access example.com's home page;

3. The LB generates a unique tag and returns it to the user along with the IP address of the proxy. The unique tag is generated as a function of (proxy server, LB, client) IP address and client's port number. To avoid the tag being forged, the tag is encrypted using proxy's public key;

4. The user then sends a HTTP request to the proxy server along with the unique tag assigned to it;

5. The proxy first decodes the unique tag, using its private/secret key and verifies the credentials present in the tag. On successful verification of the client, the proxy sends a corresponding HTTP response; otherwise, the client request/connection is dropped.

We now discuss a few attack scenarios and how our proposed scheme helps in dealing with such attacks.

1. If more than one user arrives at the proxy with the same unique tag, this situation implies that the unique tag was forged and used for another user. In that case, the user IP address and port number are monitored for possible attack traffic.

2. If an attacker manages to find the IP address of another proxy server, through another client, it is possible that the attacker might direct all the clients with a unique tag ID towards a single server. To handle this situation, the function to generate tags is dependent on the client's IP address, LB's IP address, and proxy server's IP address. Thus, only when the client arrives at the right proxy server, its request will be serviced. Thus, we make sure that the flow of traffic is regulated.

IV. Experimental Setup And Simulation Results

For our experiments, we simulate a simple network using socket programming in Java. Each component (LB, clients, proxy servers, and application servers) is a Java class running on the localhost i.e., 127.0.0.1. For our experimental setup, we have a LB that processes incoming requests from the client, and four proxy servers, which are, in turn, connected to the application servers.

Our implementation works as follows:

1. Initially, when a user request arrives at the LB, it generates a unique tag which is a function of Source/client, LB, and proxy server's IP address and encodes it into a secret tag.
2. The user request is then redirected by the LB using HTTP response 302 Found. The secret tag generated is placed as a part of the Location field in the HTTP response, along with the proxy server's IP address.
3. The redirected user request then arrives at the proxy server, where the server first extracts the unique tag and verifies the IP addresses.
4. If the secret tag is a valid one, the user request is processed; otherwise, the request is dropped. The requests will be dropped due to invalid/missing secret tags.

We simulated about 50 valid user requests by hosting client programs and sending simple HTTP GET requests for a valid document available at the Application server. Additionally, we simulated about 30 requests which were mainly attack traffic. The way we simulated the attack traffic is described below. We assume user-1 is the attacker.

1. A valid user request is sent to the LB from user-1;
2. The LB then finds a proxy server with the lowest load and returns the IP address of the proxy with a unique tag that contains user-1's IP address and port number;
3. User-1 then generates 30 requests directed to the proxy servers chosen in step-2;

In terms of performance evaluation, our primitive implementation resulted in a uniform load distribution, each proxy server having an average of about 7 users. Additionally, our proposed model was able to detect malicious/ illegitimate traffic successfully. All the valid requests were successfully redirected by the LB to available proxy servers such that the load on each proxy server was close evenly distributed. In case of attack traffic, the user requests with unique valid tags were successfully authenticated and processed by proxy servers, whereas the attack traffic without valid tags was dropped by the proxy servers.

V. FUTURE WORK

In our proposed solution, the encryption of the tag using secret key requires both the LB and the proxy server to exchange a key periodically that will be used to protect the transferred data. The encryption process may add a little bit of overhead during the initial key exchange, converting plain text to ciphertext at the LB's end and vice versa at the proxy server's end. We intend to study their effects on performance in terms of the time take to direct an incoming client to one of the proxy servers, the time it takes to process the client's HTTP request, as well as the number of false positives and negatives during DDoS detection. Additionally, we would like to compare our work with available solutions and current commercial state.

VI. CONCLUSIONS

In this paper, we propose an authentication mechanism to detect and prevent DDoS attacks in a proxy-based architecture. Our proposed technique ensures that each client request arriving at a proxy server is directed by the Load Balancer. A proxy server will only service those clients that are originally redirected by the Load Balancer. Since the Load Balancer's job is to uniformly distribute the incoming client traffic among existing proxy servers, the chances of a DDoS attack due to a huge amount of incoming traffic is mitigated. Thus, the DDoS attacks caused due to botnets can be easily handled.

REFERENCES

[1] M. Sysel and O. Doležal, "An Educational HTTP Proxy Server," In Procedia Engineering, vol. 69, 2014, pp. 128–132.

[2] M. Antonakakis et al., "Understanding the Mirai Botnet," USENIX Security Symposium, 2017, pp. 1093–1110.

[3] N. Woolf, "DDoS Attack That Disrupted Internet Was Largest of Its Kind in History, Experts Say," in The Guardian, Guardian News and Media, 26 Oct. 2016, Retrieved from: www.theguardian.com/technology/2016/oct/26/ddos-attack-dyn-mirai-botnet [accesses Oct., 2016].

[4] S. Mahrach and A. Haqiq, "DDoS Flooding Attack Mitigation in Software Defined Networks," in International Journal of Advanced Computer Science and Applications, vol. 11, 2020.

[5] K. S. Vanitha, S. V. UMA, and S. K. Mahidhar, "Distributed denial of service: Attack techniques and mitigation," International Conference on Circuits, Controls, and Communications (CCUBE), 2017, pp. 226-231, doi: 10.1109/CCUBE.2017.8394146.

[6] S. Kumar, P. Tiwari, and M. Zymbler, "Internet of Things is a revolutionary approach for future technology enhancement: a review," Journal of Big Data, vol. 6, 2019 doi: 10.1186/s40537-019-0268-2

[7] A. Baptiste, "Use a Load Balancer as a First Row of Defense Against DDOS," in Haproxy, Feb. 27, 2012, Retrieved from: www.haproxy.com/blog/use-a-load-balancer-as-a-first-row-of-defense-against-ddos/ [accesses Feb., 2012]

[8] P. Jeff, J. Blankenship, and A. Cser, "How The Mirai Botnet is Fueling Today's Largest and Most Crippling DDoS Attacks," in Akamai Forrester Research 24 Oct. 2016, Retrieved from: https://www.akamai.com/uk/en/multimedia/documents/white-paper/akamai-mirai-botnet-and-attacks-against-dns-servers-white-paper.pdf [accesses Oct., 2016]

[9] S. Venkatesan, M. Albanese, K. Amin, S. Jajodia, and M. Wright, "A Moving Target Defense Approach to Mitigate DDoS Attacks against Proxy-Based Architectures," in Proceedings of the Communications and Network Security (CNS), 2016, pp. 198-206.

[10] Q. Jia, H. Wang, D. Fleck, F. Li, A. Stavrou, and W. Powell, "Catch me if you can: A cloud-enabled DDoS defense," in Proceedings of the 44th Annual IEEE/IFIP International Conference on Dependable Systems and Networks (DSN), 2014, pp. 264 – 275.

[11] H. Wang, Q. Jia, D. Fleck, W. Powell, F. Li, and A. Stavrou, "A Moving Target DDoS Defense Mechanism," Computer Communications, vol. 46, June 2014, pp. 10 – 21.

[12] P. Wood, C. Gutierrez, and S. Bagchi, "Denial of Service Elusion (DoSE): Keeping clients connected for less," in

Proceedings of the 34th IEEE Symposium on Reliable Distributed Systems (SRDS), 2015, pp. 94–103.

[13] A. Stavrou, A. D. Keromytis, J. Nieh, V. Misra, and D. Rubenstein, "MOVE: An end-to-end solution to network denial of service," in Proceedings of the Network and Distributed System Security Symposium (NDSS), February 2005, pp. 81–96.

Towards Stable and Hybrid UDP-TCP Relay Routing for Streaming and VoIP Services

Salim Mohamed
Electrical and Computer Engineering
Michigan State University
East Lansing, USA
Email: mohame26@msu.edu

Osama Mohammed
Service Delivery and Management
Innovaway
Napoli, Italy
Email: osama.mohammed@it.ibm.com

***Abstract*—Relay or overlay routing for IP networks has been well-documented in past years. However, the implementation cost of relay solutions has not yet been conclusively identified. Dynamic-relay routing relies on periodic probing for enhanced performance while static-relay routing uses less and non-periodic probes to measure latency and packet loss. For both types, there exists considerable research focused on understanding routing dynamics. However, the literature has insufficient exploration of relay attributes, such as stability and mechanisms for reducing the relay probing burden. This paper, in particular, examines relay statistical boundaries and characteristics, such as the number of hops in a minimum delay and relay path or Hop-To-Live (HTL) count inherited from the self-similar model of Internet data. The HTL is introduced in a novel analysis to assist in predicting minimum and stable relay paths while minimizing probing overhead. For doing so, our work is based on analyzing a wide-set on $19,460$ Ping and $14,762$ IPerf paths, respectively, of a network of 140 Planetlab nodes. Further, we briefly evaluated the performance of a new hybrid User Datagram Protocol and Transmission Control Protocol (UDP-TCP) relay streaming over an inexpensive relay selection mechanism managed by a stable HTL modeling. Here, we highlight a preliminary performance of applying a layer-3 and hybrid UDP-TCP streaming a replacement for the current TCP-based stream services, such as YouTube and Voice over IP (VoIP). The main results emphasize the unnecessary repetitive probing burden over the period of 24 hours instead of a careful set of measurements for capturing and predicting relay changes. This work validates this claim by presenting that our implemented HTL-based path estimation predicts stable relay paths for the hybrid UDP-TCP streaming to overcome the high drop-rates caused by the individual TCP or UDP streaming services.**

Keywords-UDP streaming; relay characteristics; Internet measurements.

I. INTRODUCTION

A. Overview

Existing relay solutions are completely dynamic while relying on continuous probing when measuring routing changes. In contrast, static relay, routing metrics, such as latency and packet loss are not continuously measured. The ultimate goal of the static relay is reliability so that nodes remain connected. Dynamic relay, however, is used to improve the Quality of Service (QoS) periodically. The study in [11] focused on understanding Time-To-Live (TTL) changes in the IP substrate (underlay) routing. However, here, we introduce and examine the influence of a new relay (overlay) routing metric that defines the number of hops in a minimum delay relay path. For the remainder of this paper, we refer to this metric as called the Hop-To-Live (HTL). Generally, our work is a composition of two parts. The first part is an analysis of the stability characteristics of relay (overlay) routing. Preliminary, in the second part, we performed a performance evaluation of a new streaming scheme called hybrid UDP-TCP streaming. The idea here is new and simply relies on combining for each stream two distinct transport sessions. The first is a conventional TCP session for handling errors and out-of-sequence packets in the stream, and this session is only invoked whenever such an error occurs. The second session is a normal UDP session that carries the major part of the stream. The performance of our hybrid protocol is simply examined by the UDP drop rate, at which the TCP back-end protocol is involved. This evaluation was performed using relay paths determined via our proposed estimation-based path selection model. This model operates based on the HTL characteristics described in the first part. The input of this model is as a set of $19,460$ relay paths connect a 140 Planetlab nodes, and outputs a smaller set of stable relay paths for each end-to-end pair of nodes. The input relay paths represent the relay features used to derive our path estimation model, and all such paths capture only routing changes as we vary Round-Trip-Time (RTT), traffic sizes, and rates.

The main question addressed here is to determine how stable is a measurement-less model of relay paths over $24-$hours so that a single instance of underlay measurement could be reused for estimating new stable paths. The next inquiry is to look into the scale of achieved benefit when implementing our estimation model into real-time scenarios, such as a path serving for the hybrid UDP-TCP protocol.

The motivation behind using hybrid UDP-TCP instead of TCP is slightly similar to the Quick UDP Internet Connections (QUIC) protocol in [24]. QUIC is a multi-purpose application-layer protocol initially designed by Google Langley et al. [25]. Later, in 2013 QUIC was announced publicly for experimentation Langley et al. [25], and redesigned by the Internet Engineering Task Force (IETF) while still being an Internet-Draft. QUIC adds the missing reliability feature to UDP at the application-layer as opposed to being implemented at the transport-layer. Meaning, different services now can design their reliability, error-correction, privacy, and security demands at the user-space. In contrast, our hybrid, UDP-TCP does not perform maintain each of these tasks at the transport-layer while simply having UDP to forward the major stream portion, and when an error occurs, the receiving-end notifies its peer via a back-end TCP connection. This paper is neither providing a comparison between the two protocols nor a discussion on the protocol details.

Plantlab is a global and shared research network. However, many routing privileges are disabled to avoid unexpected routing between slices. Researchers at the Planetlab have designed a replacement for the well-known Unix sudo command. Vsys is a method for handling access restrictions to privileged operations. This study used an automated version of Vsys to setup all examined relay paths between end-nodes. However, defining privileges at an arbitrary granularity by filtering data between the host and guest domains is one of the tedious challenges of our work.

Relay routing introduces new implementation-concerns, such as probing overhead (cost) and its processing latency, stability, availability, and sensitivity to underlay routing changes. The lack of privilege at the IP layer in older overlay schemes required relay layers to be implemented at the user-space (application layer) instead of the kernel-space (transport-layer). One example of such schemes is the application-multicast protocol. Recently approaches like Software Defined Networks (SDNs) offer that privilege, but the probing cost remains high. The long-term boundary of our research is to develop a robust, resilient, and inexpensive layer-3 relay protocol to handle the unprecedented demand for streaming services in many circumstances, such as the global pandemics.

B. Dataset

Valuable bandwidth datasets, such as the one used in Jiang et al. [1] are private ones. Moreover, public dataset like CADIA [13] and RIP-NCC [14] do not offer large-scale and demand-based bandwidth traces. Therefore, in order to achieve meaningful bandwidth estimations on a large-scale, we used a global network of 140 nodes. These nodes are distributed across the globe as follows: North America 63.57%, South America 4.29%, Australia 3%, Asia 17.86% and Europe 12.86%. We performed a set of $311,360$ delay traces using Ping and $177,144$ bandwidth measurements via IPerf.

C. Experiments

Ping and IPerf were used to conduct measurements over $19,460$ and $14,762$ end-to-end paths, respectively in a network of $n = 140$ nodes. Ping sends its bulk of packets in four distinct sizes: 0.05, 0.1, 0.25 and 0.5 MBytes. Ping packets were also scheduled in the same order 4 times in 16 experiments. IPerf datagrams were sent at 12 distinct demand-rates as in Table II. Our diverse measurements were used to examine the HTL characteristics, and design a stable HTL-based path estimation. Having a diverse measurement interval as suggested in [11], provides more confidence in capturing possible routing changes.

D. Probing Daemon

The conducted measurements follow the exact probing abstract illustrated in [2]. The nodes were divided into a number of groups. We performed a single measurement in each group g_i where $i \in [1 \rightarrow m]$. Each prober utilizes two loops: The first, is to probe all $n-1$ nodes, and the second one is to probe unresponsive nodes again. The actual group time is: $t_i = \sum_{k=1}^{|g_i|} \lambda_i(k) + \beta_i(k)$ as $\lambda_i(k)$ and $\beta_i(k)$ are probing loops times. These times can be determined as: $\lambda_i(k) = \sum_{j=1}^{n-1} \bar{\epsilon}$ and similarly $\beta_i(k) = \eta \sum_{j=1}^{\theta_i(k)} \bar{\epsilon}$, where $\theta_i(k)$ is the number of unresponsive in the first loop. $\bar{\epsilon}$ is the average probing time in the network. $\eta = 1$ was the average count of re-probing in our case. Our probing scheme used a server-based synchronization to minimize the effect of probing conflict occurs when two daemons or more probe a particular node simultaneously. To reduce such imperfect measurements, we forced daemons to randomly probe all nodes.

Furthermore, we defined the probability of success for reducing the influence of probing conflict on the measurement accuracy. Such probability concerns $n - m$ nodes when no node was targeted simultaneously by more than one prober of m active ones. The probability of success with no conflict in probing was approximated as in [3] [4] by:

$$\Pr(\text{success}) = \prod_{i=1}^{m-1} \left(1 - \frac{i}{n-m}\right) \quad (1)$$

Here, n and m are the numbers of nodes and groups, respectively. Practically, m represents the number of active probers that can probe the network within a particular time. Therefore, m must be chosen carefully to satisfy desired success probability. Due to tedious computation when solving for an exact solution for m that satisfies a given demand of success, we can approximate the probability of success in (1) if $m \ll n$ by:

$$\Pr(\text{success}) \approx \exp\left\{-\frac{m^2}{2(n-m)}\right\} \quad (2)$$

Solving for success demand equals 70% leads to $m \approx 10$. For our network, $n = 140$, we found $m \approx 10$. Clearly, achieving 100% of success reduces m to one as expected.

E. Contribution

The major contribution of our work is in identifying short and long-term analyses of the minimum RTT relay paths, such as long-term stability as discussed in Section III and the HTL alternation sequences detailed in Section IV and Section V. Further probabilistic relay attributes, such as prevalence are studied in Section VI. For analyzing HTL characteristics, we performed $311,360$ RTT measurements for all paths in a network of 140 nodes. Through extensive analysis, we found that the HTL prevalence shares a similar behavior to the TTL prevalence studied in [11]. Therefore, we conclude that both HTL and RTT are sufficient routing metrics for predicting relay changes and thus, reducing the relay cost. This paper proposes two different schemes for using hybrid UDP-TCP as an alternative for TCP-based streaming and VoIP services and shows the difference in performance between the two schemes.

The remainder of this paper is organized as follows: Section II summarizes the importance of recent relay schemes. Dominant relay redundancy and its type are analyzed in Section VII. The proposed HTL detection scheme is briefed Section VIII. Section IX describes our proposed UDP streaming performance. Section X concludes our paper.

II. Related Research

The study in Jiang et al. [1] refers to an estimation-based relay scheme for Skype users. The skew in data density mentioned in Jiang et al. [1] is due to the lack of measurements (samples) for end-pairs, and was replaced by network tomography-based delay estimation. This approach can not be generalized and replace the probing overhead required for achieving a clear view of the network's performance. For a tomography-based estimation, our study is a counterexample, in which we found both the underlay and the relay paths are asymmetric in general. We postponed our symmetry analysis due to page limitations. Therefore, the gain of relay performance using a tomography-based scheme might not achieve the desired QoS for end-users due to the lack of delay symmetry. Researchers in [2] have used same the measurements to construct a Layer-3 forwarding scheme for data transfer at a small-scale. The considered relay paths were selected according to their HTL stability. The difficulty in performing direct probing in a large network studies [3] like [4] to show that it is possible to infer network conditions based on content distribution networks [5] with relaying. [6] is an example of such a scheme. Our study is a specific implementation of [7] and [11], in which the authors focus on examining the basic problem of QoS routing for multimedia applications by finding a path that satisfies multiple constraints. In our study we consider a new direction using UDP as relay protocol instead of TCP for YouTube and VoIP applications like Skype and Viber.

The work in [8] illustrates that IPv4 paths are more stable than IPv6 paths. This motivated us to further examine the stability of the IPv4 relay. In [9], authors highlight the importance of new schemes for predicting underlay RTTs, and that supports our claim for the need of new estimation designs for relay routing. The study in [10] uses relay path stability and symmetry characteristics to overcome the inefficiency of the relay when not considering certain underlay links. The used stability assists in finding more efficient relay paths. In contrast, we used the HTL count stability instead of the entire relay path structure in our study. Paxson in [11] examined end-to-end behaviors due to the different directions of underlay paths, which often exhibit asymmetries. The author characterized the prevalence and persistence of underlay paths. In contrast, we performed a similar analysis for relay paths. In [12], the authors examined path diversity on relay networks. They used 50 Planetlab nodes to conduct Traceroute measurements. They concluded that relay performance gains are limited by the natural diversity of redundant paths between two end-hosts in terms of underlay links, routing infrastructure, administrative control, and location. This motivated our characterization of HTL by analyzing prevalence and redundancy. The study in [17] shows that the mean of per-hop delay between parent and child nodes in a relay tree decreases as the level of the host in the relay tree increases, and this is due to the fact that current underlay routing is not optimized in-terms of delay.

III. HTL Stability

This section provides a complete identification of the HTL changes over the measurement period. The first Ping experiment is considered as a baseline since it contains all possible HTL variations for monitoring the HTL behavior. Here, we present eight HTL sets. Each set represents an average stability measure of a subset of $19,460$ relay paths for a particular HTL, meaning each set contains paths whose HTL equals the set's index. Each path of these sets was randomly traced every $[10 \rightarrow 15]$ minutes. In Figure 1, the $x-$axis indicates the probability of change, by which the paths of a set change over time, for example, $p = 1/15$ indicates a single change over 15 measurements. Each set of relay paths are described by its probability of switch p and switch type, x in (p, x) where x may represent a decrease $-$ in HTL, same $=$ HTL, or increase $+$ in HTL. The subset of paths represented by $(0, +)$ with zero probability switches to longer HTL. The subset $(0, =)$ indicates 100% change either to longer or shorter HTL. Similarly, $(0, -)$ refers to an impossible change to shorter HTL. Before discussing the actual result of this section, let's describe an ideal scenario for a stable HTL of a set of relay paths. The combination $(0, +)$ and $(0, -)$ should be maximized at zero while the $(1, =)$ should peak at one. Therefore, any analysis of this nature should approximate this ideal model in order to conclude that a set of relay paths of a particular HTL is highly stable. The IP routing dynamics, however, forces HTL to deviate in its stability.

From Figure 1, as expected, we found that for all HTL-sets, relay paths follow an exponential decay when switching to higher HTL values. The exponential curve starts to collapse as the set's HTL increases. This means that as the set's HTL increases, relay paths tend not to increase their lengths throughout the observation period. For the sets of HTL counts 2 and 3 hops, we still notice an approximation for the ideal model with a considerable decrease for all combinations. However, for the sets of HTL equal to 3 and 4 hops, the probability of always being at the same HTL is very small, and that is why the $(1, =)$ bar decreases causing a trend of decreasing HTL until peaking at $(1, -)$. By doing an overall

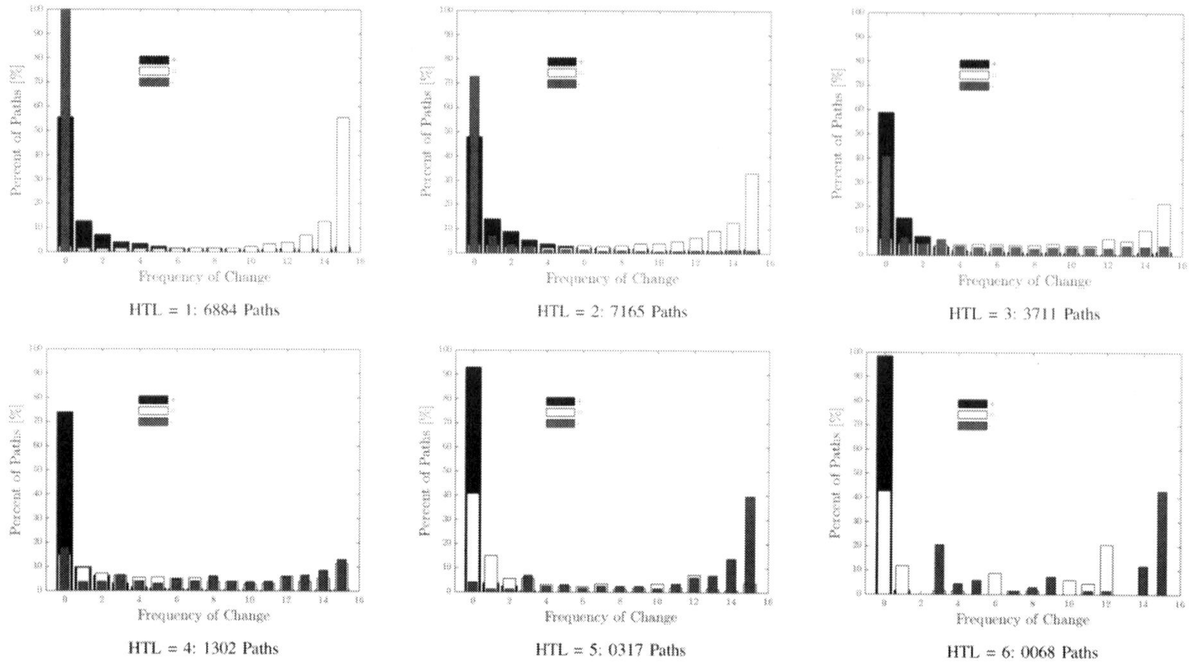

Figure 1. Relay HTL Stability.

analysis of the entire behavior of all HTL sets while focusing on $(p = 0, x)$, we conclude with three important curves. The first curve refers to the $(0, +)$ that starts near 50% in the first set and raises up toward its maximum at the eighth set. This indicates that as HTL increases, paths tend not to change to longer hops. The second curve for $(0, =)$ starts at zero percent, and with positive slope also reaches its maximum in the eighth set. That means relay paths never stay at a fixed length as HTL increases. The third curve for $(0, -)$, however, with negative slope collapsed in the sixth set. That means as HTL $\in [2 \rightarrow 6]$ increases, paths tend to reduce their lengths. The HTL stability analysis is summarized as follows: Since paths with HTL ≤ 4 hops are dominant in logical routing, we found that they either prefer to remain at constant HTL or switch to shorter HTL counts. Their tendency to reduce the number of hops is uniform, in particular for paths of HTL ≤ 3 hops. Therefore, the focus should be on HTL $\in [2 \rightarrow 4]$ hops when designing stable relay routing. Beyond 4 hops, paths are less stable in maintaining constant HTL.

IV. HTL Frequency Sequence

HTL oscillations occur due to routing changes in IP dynamics. For an underlying path, we argue that with careful path measurements at random intervals that spread over a considerable amount of time, it is possible to observe all available relay paths. This is because External Border Gateway Protocol (EBGP) only exchanges routing advertisements between adjacent Autonomous Systems (ASes), and thus, non-neighboring ASes will have no bearing on EBGP.

Since the failure of an underlay path can last for 225 seconds [18], during such a time on average, we were able to conduct measurements for some outages, and deploy better relay paths that significantly scaled up path performance as in [2]. Using the semi-Markov chain for modeling underlay fluctuations, each state of the chain depends only on a random life-time drawn independently from a state distribution. Therefore, the steady-state probability of a particular state is equal to the average time spent in that state [18]. First, each sequence of hop measurements $\mathrm{M}_s(h)$ is defined as states of a particular relay path. Each state s_i is a representation of the path at a particular granularity. From $\mathrm{M}_s(h)$, we can construct a semi-Markov process. Having $\mathrm{M}_s(h) = 1, 1, 2, 1, 2, 3, 1, 2$ means that each state number represents HTL for its observed relay path. For a an interval between consecutive measurements of 10 minutes, we can perform the following: The possible transitions within $\mathrm{M}_s(h)$ are $1 \rightarrow 1, 1 \rightarrow 2, 2 \rightarrow 1, 2 \rightarrow 3, 3 \rightarrow 1$. For state 1, its life-time is $\frac{4\times10}{70} = 0.5714$, and its transition $1 \rightarrow 2$ occurs with probability 0.75. The probability of a transition $s_1 \rightarrow s_2$ is simply defined by: $p(s_1 \rightarrow s_2) = |s_1 \rightarrow s_2||s_1 \rightarrow s_i|^{-1}$. The symbol $|\cdot|$ refers to the number of times a transition occurs. Using the later construction procedure, the semi-Markov chain for the given $\mathrm{M}_s(h)$ will converge on an actual Markov chain as we increase the number of path observations. Using $\mathrm{M}_s(h)$, each underlay path can be mapped onto a transition process composed of possible states of better relay paths. By applying such a model, we can reduce probing frequency or cost by allowing changes within pre-estimated relay paths.

Furthermore, as we vary our probing rates while conducting

a measurement sequence, we were interested in answering questions, such as what is the overall HTL miss-rate? How likely is it that a particular HTL will not be observed? To answer our first question, we introduced for each underlay path a second HTL sequence of the most probable relay HTLs so that whenever probing is required, only paths of these lengths will be investigated. This sequence is called frequency sequence $F_s(h)$. For a given underlay path r, if $M_s(h) = 3, 3, 5, 2, 4, 5$, then $F_s(h) = 3, 5, 2, 4$. Finding $F_s(h)$ for every path in our network shows that only 4.8% of $19,460$ paths with at least one alternative relay path suffer HTL miss(es). The interaction between underlay and relay substrates causes exactly 56.6% of the 4.8% relay paths to suffering from high fluctuations during our measurement period.

During analysis, there were $8,863$ paths whose $F_s(h)$ sequences demonstrated multi-hop paths (relay was always better), and suffered no HTL miss. Furthermore, an additional $5,824$ paths whose underlay candidates still included in $F_s(h)$ also suffered no HTL miss. This indicates about 75.4% of paths change their HTL within a stable $F_s(h)$ during the measurement period. By excluding fixed underlay paths, we found only 949 paths suffered HTL miss(es). Such a number is quite small compared to the total of $19,640$ paths. Figure 2 details the fraction of paths per each HTL miss.

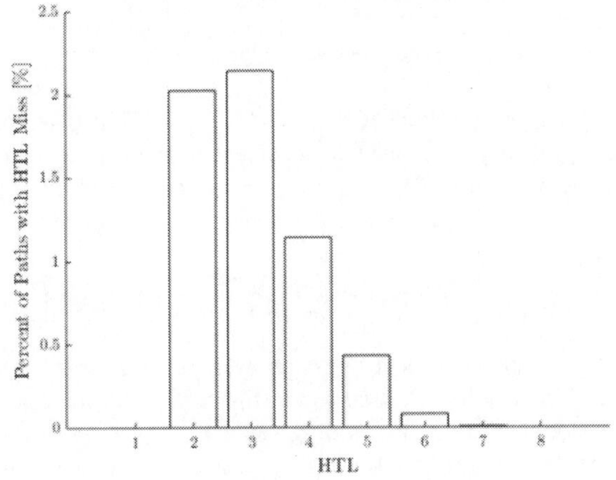

Figure 2. The Overall HTL Miss.

The probing Ping bulks were used in our measurements to create congestion and consequently to stimulate routing changes. However, despite a 2% packet loss on some paths, 2% of such paths of the total underlay paths remained constant as one-hop. The topological location of their ends might be a strong reason for such behaviour. Larger HTLs were less observed, and yet still not common in some relay paths.

V. HTL Transition Sequence

The discussion in Section IV neither investigates the nature of HTL switching, gradual or random, nor how often HTL miss(es) occur. Further, there is no strong evidence that gradual transition indicates path symmetry at the node granularity. Thus, considering time will help studying relay symmetry. The new sequence $T_s(h)$ takes time into consideration for identifying HTL miss(es) that occur between consecutive measurements. Generally, $M_s(h)$ is a sub-sequence of $T_s(h)$, and therefore, $T_s(h)$ can be generated by placing all the missing HTLs. For example, at the HTL granularity: $M_s(h) = 1, 3, 1, 2, 4, 1$, $T_s(h) = 1, \overline{2}, 3, \underline{2}, 1, 2, \overline{3}, 4, \underline{3}, \underline{2}, 1$. The upper bar indicates a miss when switching to higher HTL and vice versa. Note, HTL $= 2$ and 3 are not misses in $M_s(h)$, but they are in $T_s(h)$. Using $F_s(h)$, we can catch missing HTL counts, but not determine neither a probable miss-time nor that common path fluctuations caused a transition miss.

From $T_s(h)$, if a particular HTL is a *frequent* transition miss, such HTL count is not favorable. For a particular HTL, it can show as a miss in $T_s(h)$ while not in $F_s(h)$. For example, $M_s(h) = 2, 1, 3, 3, 2$, the corresponding $F_s(h) = 2, 3, 1$ and $T_s(h) = 2, 1, \underline{2}, 3, 3, 2$. Here we consider $T_s(h)$ as miss-free since the miss chance of HTL $= 2$ is small, 0.2. However, for $M_s(h) = 4, 3, 3, 3, 3$, $F_s(h) = 3, 4$ and $T_s(h) = 4, \underline{2}, 3, 3, 3, 3$, and despite the 0.2 small miss likelihood of HTL $= 2$, we consider such $T_s(h)$ with a miss since HTL $= 2$ is not in $F_s(h)$. For HTL = 2 hops, about 90% of our relay paths had no miss(es) during path switching. Figure 3 shows a Cumulative Distribution Function (CDF) breakdown of the transition misses for the most common relay HTLs. From such a result, we can conclude that nature of HTL switching in relay follows a gradual transition rather than a random one.

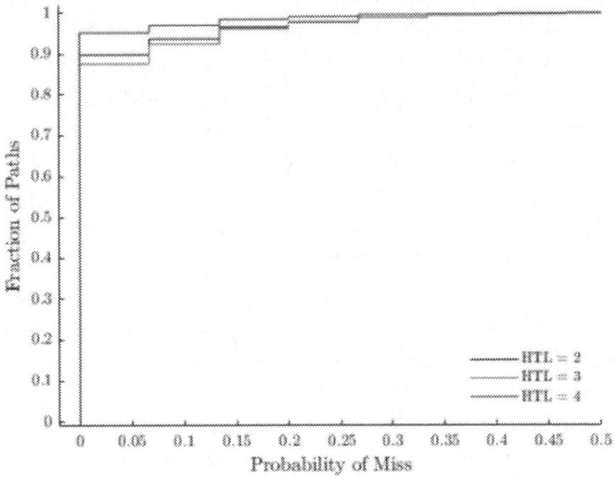

Figure 3. HTL Transition Miss Breakdown.

VI. Dominant Path Prevalence

Let us define for an underlay path r with a set of m underlay measurements: $\mathcal{U}(r) = r_1, r_2, r_2, \ldots r_m$, and another set of shorter delay relay paths: $\mathcal{O}(r) = r^1, r^2, r^1, \ldots, r^m$. Let's also introduce a dominant set $\mathcal{D}_i(r)$, where $i \in [1 \rightarrow x^*]$ as x^* is the possible number of distinct dominant sets we can observe out of m measurements for r. Each $\mathcal{D}_i(r)$ contains a subset of $\mathcal{O}(r)$ of relay paths that appear at a unique frequency of occurrence $\omega_i(r)$. For instance $\mathcal{D}_1(r)$ contains the prevalent relay paths observed at the highest frequency, $\omega_1(r)$, and $\mathcal{D}_2(r)$ encompasses paths with second highest frequency,

$\omega_2(r)$. Generally, the maximum number of dominant sets: $x^* = \arg\max_x \sum_{w=1}^{x} w \leq m$ that represent r will occur if each path of m has a unique frequency. Further, we define a source prevalence as a stronger stability measure in addition to our overall HTL stability discussion in Section III. These characteristics are manifested in the relay structure of r over time. Similarly, since the HTL transition sequence discussed in Section IV can be modeled as a Semi-Markov Process where by state represents an HTL count, and each relay path, e.g., r^1 represents a state within the process. Therefore, according to [18], we can model the steady-state likelihood by observing a state r^i to be equal to the time spent in that state.

The prevalence is defined by the steady-state likelihood of the most frequent relay observation of r during the measurement period. Generally, finding the first or second dominant relay path requires careful and frequent analysis of r at the link granularity, g_k. Similarly, in [11], we examined such characteristics at each routing granularity of the following: Node, Autonomous System (AS), city, HTL, RTT in order to determine how stable is a dominant relay path and its prediction accuracy at each granularity. Throughout our discussion, we abbreviate each granularity by g_n, g_a, g_c, g_h, g_d respectively. Using a higher level granularity for instance g_n avoids the analysis burden at g_k for example, and results in quicker estimations for r. Both g_h and g_d have not been examined in related research for estimating routing changes. Furthermore, g_h and g_d are not location dependent as are g_n, g_a and g_c. For demonstration convenience, we analyze the conditional likelihood of r^i as discussed below. For any observed dominant set, we can define $p(\mathcal{D}_i(r)|r) = \frac{\omega_i(r)}{m}$ where $i = 1, 2, \ldots x^*$ as the steady-state likelihood for any relay path in $\mathcal{D}_i(r)$ or prevalence. Here, and again, $\mathcal{D}_i(r)$ considers all relay paths in $\mathcal{O}(r)$ appear with maximum frequency or ω_1. The size of each dominant set $|\mathcal{D}_i(r)|$ represents the prevalence redundancy as explained in Section VII. Figure 4 shows only our cumulative distribution of prevalence of the first dominant set of all paths in our study at each granularity. For example, at g_n, approximately 51%, on the y-axis was dominated by at least one path with a prevalence of 75%, on the x-axis. Surprisingly, our result was very close to [11], in which 49% of underlay paths had prevalence equal to 80%. This indicates two important points: (1) That our measurements and results is strong enough in order to be generalized, and (2) Having a large-scale measurement allows the capturing of stable view of relay behavior. Similar to [11], we find 30% of our measurements are stable or long-lived because they exhibit a prevalence of one. For g_c and g_a, our spread in prevalence is also narrow as expected in [11], because Planetlab is not diverse enough at such granularities.

In contrast to [18], Figure 4 shows path fluctuations at g_a, and implies changes at g_c and vice-verse for both dominant sets, since prevalence at g_c is always strictly below the one at g_a. More strongly, since g_n curve is strictly above g_a, g_c and g_h, with 100% any changes at g_n are as well reflected at any other granularity. This is because the same lack of diversity within Planetlab makes it rare to find nodes belonging to different ASes within the same city or vice versa. In general, having large prevalence medians, 0.75 at g_n, and 0.81 at both g_c and g_a indicates a wide spread in distribution. The prevalence at g_h is strictly less than either of the remaining granularities as expected, and so a change in a path at g_n, g_c or g_a will always be captured by a HTL change. The only missing fact, however, in order to rely on the HTL count for estimating path changes, is the the percentage of error when facing a no change scenario as Section VIII discusses.

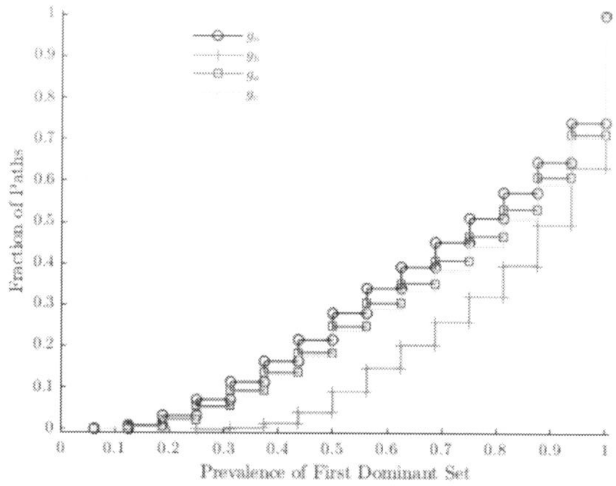

Figure 4. Dominant Path Prevalence.

Similarly, each source of $s \in S = \{1, 2, \ldots N\}$ is associated with an overall prevalence that considers every underlay path r starts from s and in $\mathcal{R}_s = \{r | r : s \rightarrow s' \quad \forall s' \neq s \wedge \exists \mathcal{D}_1(r)\}$. Therefore, source prevalence is calculated as following:

$$p(s|\mathcal{R}_s) = \frac{\sum_{r \in \mathcal{R}_s} \omega_1(r)}{m|\mathcal{R}_s|} \quad (3)$$

The source prevalence in (3) is an average measure of relay routing stability for a source node. Higher $p(s|\mathcal{R}_s)$ indicates a stable dominant relay forwarding via s. Both path and source prevalence are considered as long-term stability characteristics. The source prevalence gives an overall view of the first dominant set of a source s concerning all remaining nodes. The changes near a particular source will affect the prevalence of that source alone [11]. The far path fluctuations in a network will affect all sources not only a particular one [11]. The concept of source prevalence in our study follows that of a similar study [11]. Since underlay routing is not optimized in terms of RTT, oftentimes it is usual to observe that paths out of the same node follow produced disjointed links early on. However, given that our study is an analysis of the shortest relay delay paths, such paths were not expected to be disjoint near their sources, but further into the network. Our analysis shows that on average nodes have 70% of their paths as considerably stable. The prevalence of the second dominant set converges earlier than the first set since being seen as a dominant path reduces the chance of a second dominant one appearing.

Generally, having an underlying path with an extremely small prevalence, for example, the minimum value in our study is 0.0625 indicates a short-lived relay path. However, no relay path showed a minimum below 0.0625 in our study. Low prevalence generally does not exist in underlay routing as [11] confirmed. This is because both intra-domain and inter-domain routing helps to maintain paths with fewer fluctuations. For relay routing, however, the measurement wide view makes such a low prevalence impossible.

VII. Dominant Path Redundancy

Following Section VI, and for reliable relay routing, applications should incorporate a multiplicity of dominant paths, for example as in the dominant set: $|\mathcal{D}_i(r)| = \phi_{\mathcal{D}_i}(r)$. Furthermore an underlay path r with seven relay observations, such as $r^1, r^1, r^2, r^2, r^2, r^1, r^3$ has only two dominant sets with $\phi_{\mathcal{D}_1}(r) = 2$ and $\phi_{\mathcal{D}_2}(r) = 1$. In the dominant set $\mathcal{D}_i$, we

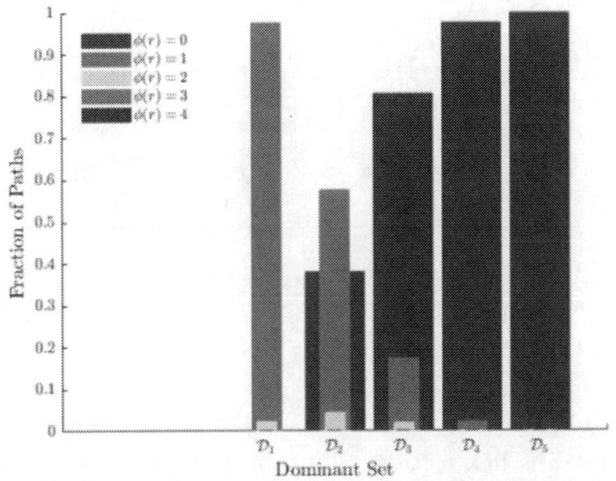

Dominant Relay Path Redundancy

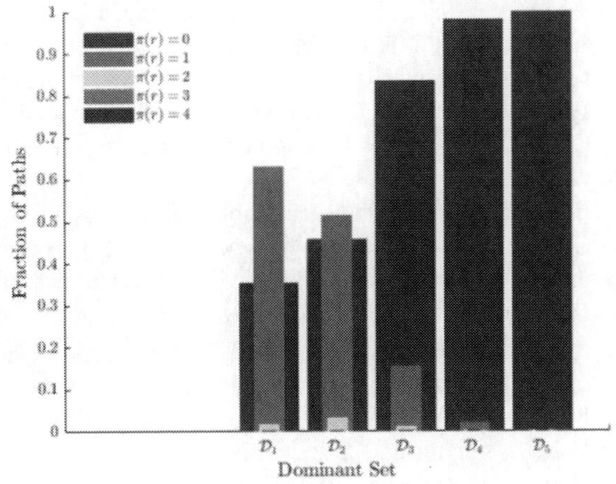

Dominant Relay Path Type

Figure 5. Redundancy and Type of Relay Paths.

were interested in how many paths in $\mathcal{D}_i$ were relay paths. Such a metric $\pi_{\mathcal{D}_i}(r)$ indicates how often relay routing is willing to replace r by better relay paths. For simplicity, we only used HTL to analyze dominant redundancy and type at g_h. Figure 5 shows categorical histograms of both $\phi_{\mathcal{D}_i}(r)$ and $\pi_{\mathcal{D}_i}(r)$, respectively. Clearly, for $\mathcal{D}_i(r)$, $\phi_{\mathcal{D}_i}(r)$ can not be zero as there is always at least one path in $\mathcal{D}_i$. As expected we observed a linear increase in $\phi_{\mathcal{D}_i}(r) = 0$ for $i \in [2 \rightarrow 5]$ as dominant sets tend to be empty for smaller path prevalence. Similarly, $\phi_{\mathcal{D}_i}(r) = 1$ decreases as path prevalence decreases. Note, the summation of the four bars at each dominant set equals one. Figure 5 shows that $\pi_{\mathcal{D}_i}(r)$ follows a similar pattern to $\phi_{\mathcal{D}_i}(r)$ but at different rates. Further, Figure 5 shows that 60% of examined paths have exactly one relay path in their $\mathcal{D}_1$ while 30% have no alternative other than the underlay paths in $\mathcal{D}_1$.

VIII. Detection of HTL Changes

The discussion in Section VI shows at g_n, nearly 50% of our $19,460$ examined source-destination paths, are dominated by a single path with prevalence equal to 0.75. The question now is: Can HTL be used by relay nodes in relation to routing changes without any probing overhead? There are many reasons for such a correlation. Detecting relay changes permits nodes to update performance metrics, such as RTT and bandwidth. Therefore, for measurement-based routing, recognizing routing changes is important for future performance estimations.

Current relay systems do not incorporate the hop-count or HTL in their relay headers. This information could be as helpful as the TTL is in the underlay layer. For applications, it could be more important to know the HTL rather than TTL as they could adjust HTL according to their QoS demand. Smaller TTL does not ensure smaller HTL, which means small processing delays of the relay overhead. Furthermore, for end-nodes, a few link changes do not indicate a change in the relay routing as long as such changes still occur between the same relay nodes. Therefore, an additional HTL field should be included in the relay header in order for end-nodes to detect relay changes.

The growth of the Internet might cause routing to exceed the maximum TTL value, 255. Because of the current existence of relay paths with HTL beyond 3 hops in our small network of 140 nodes, we found a widespread distribution in relay link consumption near 70 links, which exceeds the default TTL of 64 Backes et al. [15] and [16]. Hence, relay routing might not improve routing performance in the near future. While forwarding a relay packet via a relay path, the original IP packet is unmodified except for decreasing the TTL. Therefore, for long relay paths, an initial TTL might reach zero before reaching the final destination, and the packet will be dropped. To solve such an issue for the future relay Internet, relay nodes can modify the TTL in the original IP header by allowing nodes to provide a layer-2 update on IP. Via this method relay nodes can access the original IP header to increment the TTL count when necessary. A question raised by such a mechanism is: When should a relay node modify TTL? The relay node increments TTL when the HTL count has not reached zero. There is no need for copying out the original TTL from a selected packet (uniform model) to the outer (relay) IP header before checking and decrementing TTL [20].

The proposed HTL mechanism for detecting relay changes requires including the HTL field in the encapsulated relay header. As a result, relay nodes can determine if a change has occurred without extra probing. The remaining of this section discussed our results for using HTL to detect relay changes. Table I summarizes all associated False-Positive (FP), False-Negative (FN), and total errors when relying on relay routing at g_h for predicting actual relay changes. The FN rate can be reported at every granularity. For instance, when HTL equals 2 hops of two consecutive measurements, corresponding relay paths can be: $r^1 := a \rightarrow b \rightarrow c$ and $r^2 := a \rightarrow d \rightarrow c$, although such a change can not be detected at g_h granularity.

The HTL does not result in FP at g_n since any no-change in the nodes involved in a relay path will not be reported as a change by HTL. However, at g_a or g_c HTL can report a FP when HTL changes but the relay path is still constant at those granularities. The FP in our dataset was zero even at g_a and g_c since the Planetlab slice was not dense enough at both granularities.

TABLE I. HTL CHANGE DETECTION

Granularity	FN %	FP %	Error %
g_n	41	0.00	15
g_a	35	0.00	12
g_c	33	0.00	10

IX. HTL-Based Hybrid UDP-TCP Streaming

Briefly, this section summarizes our approach to handling UDP-TCP streaming requests. From Figure 6, the controller passes the requester ID to a relay path selection, and receives back all possible stable bandwidth relay paths. The controller then compares the performance of the selector's returned sub-topology in order to choose a relay scheme for the request.

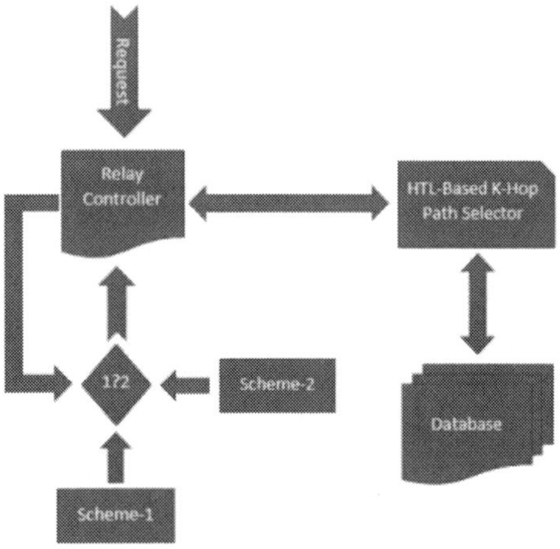

Figure 6. HTL-Based UDP-TCP Request Handling.

A. Bandwidth

Bandwidth is a complex metric measured by tools, such as the listed [13]. None of these tools are robust and scalable. The IPerf is still considered a benchmark in many studies. In our study, IPerf is used to evaluate the UDP bandwidth of all-pairs using 12 rate-demands. We assigned a UDP stream for each rate-demand as detailed in Table II. For each desired rate, all IPerf clients generated the same traffic size for their IPerf servers. The higher rate-demands were attempts to reduce the effect of cross-traffic during our measurements by overloading each examined underlay path with a back-to-back flow of datagrams. Generally, each rate-demand is bounded by the client's network hardware. For ensuring consistency in our measurements, IPerf used its default datagram size of 1500 Bytes as Maximum Transmission Unit (MTU) in order to treat datagrams as packets. However, few clients with multiple interfaces vary their average datagram size due to the distinct hardware of each interface. The average MTU by each node in our Iperf experiments was 1500 Bytes.

TABLE II. UDP RATE-DEMAND AND TRAFFIC

Rate-Demand [Mbps]	Traffic [MBytes]
0.5	0.5
2	4
3	6
5	8
10	10
5	20
5	40
10	80
10	100
10	200
10	400
10	800

For a rate-demand set of link measurements, $\mathcal{L}$, a maximum transmission rate of an egress-interface of a link l is: $r_l^* = \arg \underset{\forall i}{max} \quad r_l^i$, where $i \in \mathcal{L}$. The maximum rate r^* is often called link capacity. The link capacity is always the upper-bound of the available bandwidth $b_l \leq r_l^*$ on a link. Similarly, for path p of $\mathcal{P}$ samples, $r_p^* = \arg\ max \quad \underset{l \in p}{min} \quad r_l^*$, and consequently, $b_p \leq r_p^*$. Instead of locating a bottleneck with an unnecessary link overhead, an end-to-end bandwidth measurement for a path p should focus on the bottleneck capacity in order to obtain b_p. This study uses IPerf to measure the available bandwidth all-paths conditioned by the given drop-rate threshold τ.

For many applications, an acceptable packet loss in UDP streams is %1. We evaluated our bandwidth under different drop-rates, and examined the change in our measurements as τ varies. For a path p, we defined $b_p = \arg \underset{i}{max} \quad \{r_i | d_p <= \tau\}$ where $i \in \mathcal{P}$. In our study, the number of samples of each path, $|\mathcal{L}| = 12$ as detailed in Table II. However, evaluating b_p is based-on IPerf accuracy but is expensive in probing. We call b_p in our results an expensive bandwidth. Figure 7 shows the cumulative gain of the expensive b_p as τ varies for all $147,62$ paths. The increase in bandwidth refers to

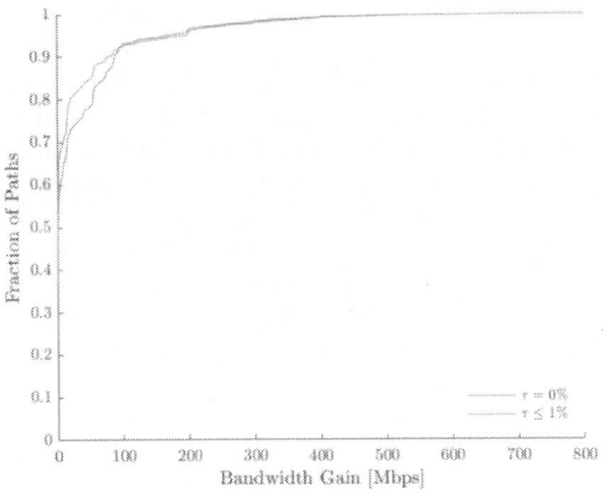

Figure 7. The Expensive Bandwidth Gain.

the difference between the underlay and the relay b_p. The slow CDF convergence indicates more paths gaining more bandwidth using our the relaying scheme outlined above. From Figure 7, we noticed that few paths gained higher relay bandwidths as τ increases. However, the range of $[0 \rightarrow 100]$ Mbps seems to be the dominant bandwidth gain.

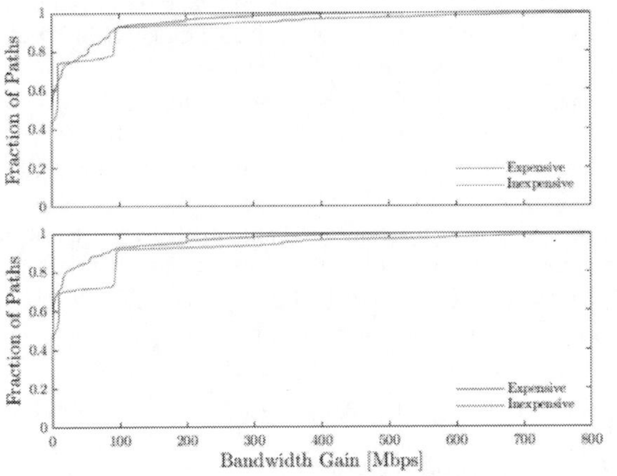

Figure 8. The Expensive vs. Inexpensive Bandwidth Gain (The Upper for $\tau \leq 0$, and Lower for $\tau \leq 1$).

Finding accurate bandwidth estimations requires more careful probing. However, streaming services like YouTube and VoIP applications, such as Skype and Viber might not accommodate such schemes. This paper provides a less expensive probing relaying scheme by choosing a smaller set of demand-rates to evaluate bandwidth. For a Youtube rate-demand, a centralized controller will receive a request from a client with a specific demand, and then probe stable HTL relay paths within the network at the requested demand-rate. This scheme is less expensive in terms of the probing overhead than the previous one. In Figure 8, we compared the performance from Figure 7, in which bandwidth gains were determined for each rate-demand in Table II with only a single set of measurements at a user rate-demand of 800 Mbps.

Figure 8 compares the performance of the expensive scheme in Figure 7, with the inexpensive relay scheme. Our second scheme focused on finding relay paths that offered bandwidth gain and were based on a single rate-demand without the need for the exact bandwidth. However, the expensive scheme used more demand-rates to obtain more accurate bandwidths for all paths before exploring relay gains. Figure 8 indicates that as we reduce our drop-rate demand, or equivalently, increasing τ, we noticed within $[0 \rightarrow 100]$ Mbps, as expected the performance of the inexpensive surpasses its counterpart as the CDF of the later converses earlier. The inexpensive scheme considered only the rate-demand, 800 Mbps, or the maximum possible for a node. However, the actual bandwidth for this node might be below such a high rate-demand. From Figure 8, we concluded that using a less-probing overhead, quickly the inexpensive relay scheme is able to serve UDP-TCP streams at higher rates without exactly determining the available bandwidth for each path. Further, within our examined network, we found that the bandwidth range $[0 \rightarrow 100]$ is the common demand-rate.

B. Hybrid UDP-TCP Success

The use of UDP for streaming instead of TCP is a tradeoff between speed and the handling of the datagram loss. The UDP receiver will discard any duplicate datagrams. There are many studies that analyzed the multi-path [20] [21] or multi-session [22] and [23] TCP performance. For instance, the Multi-Path TCP (MP-TCP) detailed in [19] is a protocol that handles load-balancing and traffic forwarding via multiple paths. The Datagram Congestion Control Protocol (DCCP) described in the Request for Comments (RFC) 4340 can serve as a general congestion-control mechanism for UDP applications to avoid congested links at the IP layer. There are many possible solutions for unreliable connections like UDP streams. First, a joint UDP-TCP connection can solve this issue when the TCP is used as a back-end session for the dropped UDP datagram, while the major portion of the stream still uses UDP. The second solution is to use a similar approach to MP-TCP. A Multi-Path UDP (MP-UDP) allows a UDP sender to duplicate its stream on multiple paths, and the receiver then has a better chance of recovering dropped datagrams. QUIC in [24] duplicates important datagrams but using a single UDP path.

The later solution might introduce duplicate traffic between its receiver and sender as with online-games. For physically compromised client-server connections, we have been trying to determine the likelihood of obtaining a relay path with a minimum drop-rate given a particular rate-demand. Through this path, a UDP client will receive the entire stream without involving TCP to resend incorrect or lost datagrams. Figure 9 shows a relationship between such a likelihood and the rate-demand. The increase in the likelihood of occurs as we raise the rate-demand. This because we find that the current underlay routing is prepared to send UDP streams only at low demand-rates in order to avoid high drop-rates. Therefore, as the demand-rate increases, packets start to experience more loss, and consequently, hybrid relay routing is a suitable solution for such an issue.

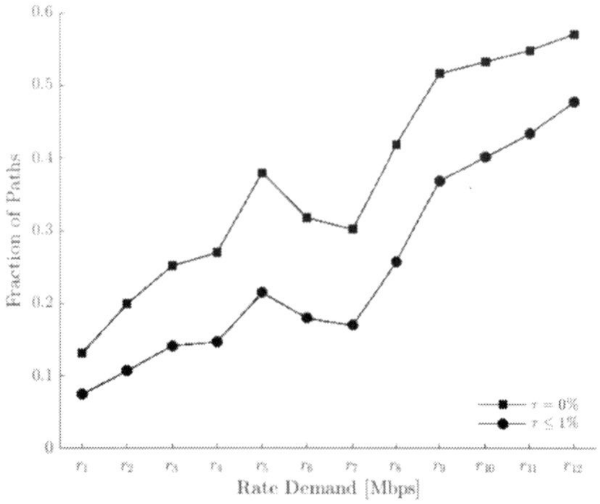

Figure 9. The Likelihood of Successful UDP-TCP Streaming.

X. Conclusion and Future Work

Recently, the speed, at which emerging technologies demand Internet access is higher than the one of developing Internet infrastructure. Relay routing is a principal solution proposed to handle such obstacles at a lower-cost for over a decade. However, relay routing still lacks studies that perform relay characteristics exploration for enhancing performance. This study demonstrates that relay paths are more stable in terms of HTL, and results show that an HTL-based relay path selection assists in reducing the search overhead for better paths as services demand. Furthermore, some services are short-time lived ones, and looking for better paths in large networks might be disadvantageous, especially when the searching time is longer than the service life-time. Hence, our work examines characteristics, such as the relay HTL count to assist in predicting minimum and stable relay paths while minimizing probing overhead. The paper is an attempt for minimizing the propping overhead in overlay schemes and detailing many statistical boundaries for the relay forwarding by analyzing a wide-set of real-time measurements. Our work recommends that an HTL-based relay path prediction is able to determine future paths that reduce drop-rates in streaming services when high transmission-rates are demanded. Further, such an enhancement occurs while reducing probing overhead for minimum delay routing demands by using a single set of measurements. This reduction in probing is a result of the self-similarity model of Internet data.

The study shows that relay paths with HTL ≤ 4 hops are dominant, and they either tend to remain at constant HTL or switch to shorter HTL counts. Their tendency to reduce the number of hops is uniform, Therefore, the focus should be on HTL $\in [2 \rightarrow 4]$ hops when designing stable relay routing. Beyond 4 hops, paths have less stable HTL models. From $19,460$ relay paths, we found $8,863$ paths whose relay option is always better than the underlay routing, and remain within a stable HTL model. An additional $5,824$ paths whose underlay candidates still included also present a miss-free HTL model. Meaning, in total about 75.4% of paths switch their HTLs within stable models during our measurement period. Thus, by excluding constant underlay paths, only 949 paths suffered HTL miss(es). We also concluded that 30% of our measurements are strongly stable or long-lived as they exhibit a prevalence of one. However, regarding the detection of relay changes, the HTL metric was able to detect relay changes with an error of 15%.

For large scale-networks, we find that instead of focusing on exact bandwidth estimates, our second streaming scheme shows that it is highly possible to find other relay paths that can serve a demand-rate quickly. Briefly, we evaluated the performance of a new hybrid UDP-TCP relaying using our HTL-managed relay path selection mechanism. More, precisely, the HTL path modeling was implemented to guide a less-probing path selection for the hybrid UDP-TCP streaming. Here, we simply highlighted a preliminary performance analysis of using the hybrid UDP-TCP streaming carried over layer-3 data-forwarding relay as a replacement for the current TCP-based stream services, such as YouTube and VoIP. Currently, we are expanding our work to design a QUIC counterpart composed of a hybrid UDP-TCP in order to eliminate the introduced QUIC overhead at the user-space while maintaining error-handling, packet security, privacy, and reliability at the kernel-space via the current TCP protocol.

In summary, our analysis emphasizes that a repetitive probing burden for 24−hours is unnecessary. Instead, a 24−hours of a careful measurement set is suitable to capture essential path characteristics. The validation of this claim has been justified by presenting that our implemented HTL-based path estimation predicts stable relay paths for the hybrid UDP-TCP streaming to overcome the high drop-rates caused by the individual TCP or UDP streaming.

References

[1] J. Jiang et al., "VIA: Improving Internet Telephony Call Quality Using Predictive Relay Selection," SIGCOMM, pp. 286–299, 2016.

[2] S. Mohamed, S. Das, S. Biswas, and O. Mohammed, "On The Significance of Layer-3 Traffic Forwarding," WWIC, Bologna, Italy, pp. 170-181, 2019

[3] J. Kim, A. Chandra and Weissman, "OPEN: Passive Network Performance Estimation for Data-intensive Applications," Technical Report, pp.8-41, 2008.

[4] A. Su, D. Choffnes, A. Kuzmanovic, and F. Bustamante, "Drafting Behind Akamai, Travelocity-Based Detouring," In Proceedings of SIGCOMM, pp. 435–446, 2006.

[5] http://www.akamai.com, retrieved: 09-21-2020.

[6] D. Choffnes and F. Bustamante, "On the Effectiveness of Measurement Reuse for Performance-Based Detouring," INFOCOM, pp. 693-701, 2009.

[7] Z. Wang and J. Crowcroft, "Quality of Service Routing for Supporting Multimedia Applications," IEEE JSAC, pp. 1228-1234, 1996.

[8] F. Golkar, T. Dreibholz, and A. Kvalbein, "Measuring and Comparing Internet Path Stability in IPv4 and IPv6," In Proceedings of the 5th IEEE International Conference on the Network of the Future (NoF), pp. 1-5, 2014.
[9] R. Fontugne, J. Mazel, and K. Fukuda, "An Empirical Mixture Model for Large-Scale RTT Measurements," In Proceedings, IEEE INFOCOM, pp. 2470-2478, 2015.
[10] A. Lareida, D. Meier, T. Bocek, and B. Stiller, "Towards Path Quality Metrics for Overlay Networks," IEEE 41st Conference on Local Computer Networks, pp. 156–159, 2016.
[11] V. Paxson, "End-to-End Internet Packet Dynamics," In Proceedings of SIGCOMM, pp. 139-152, 1997.
[12] J. Han, D. Watson, and F. Jahanian, "An Experimental Study of Internet Path Diversity," IEEE Transactions on Dependable and Secure Computing, pp. 273-288, 2006.
[13] https://www.caida.org, retrieved: 09-21-2020.
[14] https://www.ripe.net, retrieved: 09-21-2020.
[15] M. Backes, "On the Feasibility of TTL-Based Filtering for DRDoS Mitigation," RAID, pp 303-322, 2016.
[16] "IP Option Numbers: The Current Recommended Default TTL for Internet Protocol is 64 [RFC791] and [RFC1122]," https://www.iana.org/assignments/ip-parameters/ip-parameters.xml, retrieved: 09-21-2020.
[17] S. Fahmy and M. Kwon, "Characterizing Overlay Multicast Networks and Their Costs," IEEE/ACM Transactions on Networking, pp. 373-386, 2007.
[18] V. Paxson, "Measurements and Analysis of End-to-End Internet Dynamics," Ph.D. Thesis, pp. 1-386, 1997.
[19] A. Ford, C. Raiciu, M. Handley, and O. Bonaventure, "TCP Extensions for Multipath Operation with Multiple Addresses", Internet-draft, IETF, pp. 1-64, 2011, retrieved: 09-21-2020.
[20] V. Tran, Q. Coninck, B. Hesmans, R. Sadre, and O. Bonaventure, "Observing real Multipath TCP Traffic," Journal of Computer Communications, pp. 114-122, 2016.
[21] L. Chaufournier, A. Ali-Eldin, and P. Sharma, "Performance Evaluation of Multi-Path TCP for Data Center and Cloud Workloads," ICPE, pp. 13-24, 2019.
[22] A. Baldini, L. De Carli and F. Risso, "Increasing Performances of TCP Data Transfers Through Multiple Parallel Connections," ISCC, pp. 630-636, 2009.
[23] T. Nguyen and S. Cheung, "Multimedia Streaming Using Multiple TCP Connections," PCCC, pp. 215-223, 2005.
[24] J. Iyengar and M. Thomson, "QUIC: A UDP-Based Multiplexed and Secure Transport," Internet-Draft, https://tools.ietf.org/html/draft-ietf-quic-transport-29, retrieved: 09-21-2020.
[25] A, Langley et al., "The QUIC Transport Protocol: Design and Internet-Scale Deployment," SIGCOMM, pp. 183-196, 2017.

Towards Securing Big Data on Software Defined Network: Performance Aware Architecture Design

Ahmed Mohammed Alghamdi
Department of Software Engineering
College of Computer Science and Engineering
University of Jeddah
Jeddah, Saudi Arabia
E-mail: amalghamdi@uj.edu.sa

Abstract—**Big data security and privacy have been the main concern because many organizations have started to depend on big data for their operations. Big data refers to a large amount of structure and unstructured data that has been defined differently, but, in general, this term refers to the collection of data sets, which has special characteristics. Big data security faces the need to protect sensitive data by using different technologies and policies. It has been argued that there is no comprehensive security solution for big data, however, to achieve this comprehensive solution, parts of big data should be protected and secured. In addition, Software Defined Network (SDN) has gained more interest due to its advantages in improving network management, as well as monitoring with more programmability and better network resource utilization. Many researches have been done in this field, but the trade-off between security and performance has not been considered, especially considering SDN. In this paper, an architecture design is proposed for big data security, which considers security and performance trade-off. The proposed architecture is based on giving each part of big data the proper security mechanism to protect them efficiently, which not only improves the performance, but also saves resources.**

Keywords-Big Data; Big data security; Hadoop; Software Defined Network.

I. Introduction

In recent years, big data has become increasingly one of the hot topics in Information Technology (IT) research society. This importance comes from the various data usages as well as its analysis and huge size. According to Big Data statistics, data has increased 300 times to be 40,000 Exabytes in 2020 and the Big Data market is currently worth $138.9 billion [1]. The uses of big data and its analysis have attracted information science researchers, decision-makers in public and private sectors, healthcare systems, and IT companies. In addition, Software Defined Networking (SDN) has been recently gaining more interest due to many features that are offered by SDN, which improves the network management and resource utilization. According to Statistics MRC, the "World Software Defined Networking (SDN) Market accounted for $10.88 billion in 2015 and is projected to rise to $134.51 billion by 2022 at a CAGR of 43.2% from 2015 to 2022", which is very high [2].

SDN provides many advantages including programmable network access, large and complex data traffic management, reduced network hardware capital and operating costs, and personalized data control, which has inspired companies to embrace this technology. SDN is a layered network architecture offering unparalleled programmability, automation, and network control by the ramification of the network's control plane and data plane [2]. The network knowledge and states are logically centralized in the SDN architecture, and the underlying network infrastructure for network applications is abstracted. One of the key advantages of this approach is that it offers a more organized software framework for the creation of network-wide abstractions while simplifying the data plane capacity.

Big data refers to any large amount of structured and unstructured data. There are various explanations of big data via Vs, which range from 3 to 6 Vs. Typically, 5 Vs used to characterize the big data including; volume, velocity, variety, veracity, and value. The volume is the data size; velocity is the speed of generating and changing the data; variety is the data in many forms; veracity is accuracy and validity of the data; and value, which provides output from large data set [1][3][4]. Big data have many challenges and difficulties due to their characteristics. It is also important to emphasize that big data can be used for critical decision-making and sensitive tasks; as a result, data trustworthiness is a critical requirement [5]. Data must be protected from unauthorized access and modifications, accurate, complete, and up-to-date. Big data security can be seen from three main aspects including; confidentiality, integrity, and availability. Many components of big data need to be secure including; the data itself during storage, transferring, processing, and the value extracted from these data. Also, other hardware and software components as well as the cloud providers and big data platforms. However, a comprehensive security solution is difficult to achieve in big data.

The rest of this paper is structured as follows. Section 2 discusses big data definitions, characteristics, as well as SDN related aspects. In Section 3, a literature review of big data security challenges and solutions will be shown, as well as SDN-big data related researches. In Section 4, the proposed architecture will be displayed and described. Section 5, evaluation and comparative study are discussed and compared. Finally, in Section 6, we present the conclusion as well as the future works.

II. BACKGROUND

In this section, two main aspects of our research will be presented to give an overview of them including big data and SDN as the following:

A. Big Data

Although the term "Big Data" has become increasingly common, its meaning is not always clear. Big data has many definitions and explanations, but in general, this term refers to the collection of data sets which has special characteristics including big volume and variety, as a result, it is difficult to deal with such data by using traditional tools of data management and processing. According to Gartner IT glossary [6], the term big data is defined as: High-volume, high-velocity and/or high-variety information assets that demand cost-effective, innovative forms of information processing that enable enhanced insight, decision making, and process automation. Similarly, Tec America Foundation [7] defines big data as follows: Big data is a term that describes large volumes of high velocity, complex and variable data that require advanced techniques and technologies to enable the capture, storage, distribution, management, and analysis of the information. In terms of the big data characteristics, it often characterizes by three factors: volume, velocity, and variety refer to them as 3 Vs. However, many researches claimed that big data could be characterized by many Vs, usually ranging from 3 to 6 Vs. In this paper, the 5 Vs will be used to characterize big data, as shown in Figure 1, include the following:

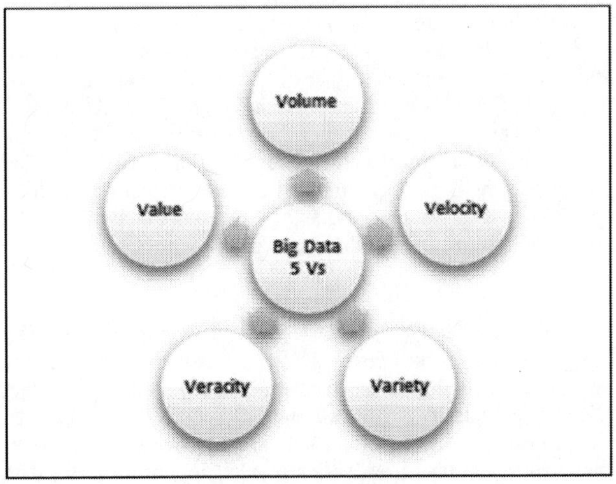

Figure 1. Big Data 5 V's.

1. **Volume**: It refers to the data collected and stored in many distributed systems. It is usually a huge amount of data, which could exceed Exabyte, which can be processed to extract valuable knowledge. The more the data volume increases, the more difficulties for processing with considering performance.
2. **Value**: It is the most important feature of big data that extracting the data value from big data within a specific amount of time. Sometimes the extracted value is more important than the data itself and it has meaning and uses more than using the data before processing.
3. **Veracity**: The validity and accuracy of the collected data have major importance. The quality of Big Data may be good, bad, or undefined due to data inconsistency, incompleteness, ambiguities, and latency. As a result, extracting knowledge or values cannot be occurred from invalid or inaccurate data or might lead to false interpretation. Because of that, collected data need to be checked and any doubt about gathering data should be removed.
4. **Variety**: It refers to the variety of the data types; data could be structured, unstructured, and semi-structured. It also could be internal or external; the internal data is gathered from internal resources in the organization, whereas the external data is gathered from sources. This variety allows processors to extract as interesting as varied information about a specific topic.
5. **Velocity**: It refers to how fast data is being produced and changed and the speed with which data must be received, understood, and processed. Big data does not only rely on static record but it also uses real-time streams and without storage. Processing big data has to be able to generate and extract the results in a few seconds or few milliseconds. Even a few seconds is too late for some critical applications.

Despite the importance of big data, this can lead to a revaluation in organizations and enterprises. The previous five criteria brought the needs to find tools and mechanisms for efficiently processing and analyzing the data. In terms of the big data systems, Hadoop is one of the most popular big data systems, which used to store and process big data. Hadoop is an open-source software used for big data, because of its ability to deal with a very big amount of distributed data. According to The Apache Software Foundation [8], Hadoop is defined as: A framework that allows for the distributed processing of large data sets across clusters of computers using simple programming models. Hadoop has many modules including the following [8]:

- **Hadoop Common**: The common utilities that support the other Hadoop modules.
- **Hadoop Distributed File System (HDFS):** A distributed file system that provides high-throughput access to application data. Hadoop uses a block-structured distributed file system for storing a large amount of data called the Hadoop Distributed File System (HDFS). All the individual files in HDFS are divided into blocks with fixed sizes. A cluster of machines with storage capacity is used to store these blocks. The major components of HDFS are NameNode, DataNode, and BackUpNode.

- **Hadoop YARN**: A framework for job scheduling and cluster resource management.
- **Hadoop MapReduce**: A YARN-based system for parallel processing of large data sets.

Big data has many security issues and challenges as well as privacy concerns, which must be taken into consideration before building a big data environment. The following are some of the most important challenges that should be considered when dealing with big data:

- Access Control
- Communication Security
- Data Integrity
- Computations Security
- Privacy
- Random Distribution
- Cloud Security
- Hadoop Security
- End-Point input validation and filtering

Traditional security solutions are insufficient when dealing with big data to ensure security and privacy. Encryption techniques, access permissions, firewalls, transport layer security can be broken. For these reasons, advanced techniques and technologies are needed to protect, monitor, and audit big data in terms of data, applications, and infrastructures.

B. Software Defined Network (SDN)

SDN has been defined as an emerging network architecture designed to improve and simplify network management as well as improve network resource utilization. SDN can be viewed in three different layers including data plane, control plane, and application plane. This separation of network devices from their management enables the network control to be programmable, independently developed, and have a flexible design compared to the traditional network architectures [2]. The following Figure 2 shows the SDN architecture.

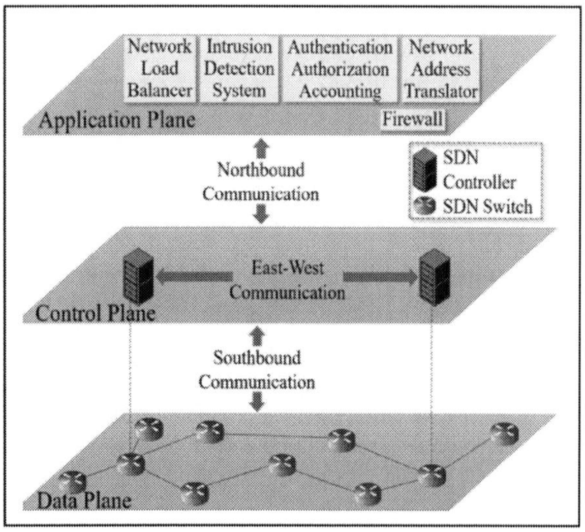

Figure 2. SDN Architecture [9].

The first layer of the SDN architecture is a data plane that includes switches, whether physical and virtual switches, that are considered as forwarding devices. The switches give a view of the programmable flow tables that can describe an operation related to a particular flow for each packet. The second layer of the SDN architecture is the control plane that moves the control logic to an external body, called the SDN controller, which lies within the architecture's control plane. The controller is a software interface that has a full view of the network and the ability to make optimal routing decisions, thereby increasing the visibility of the network. The network is programmable by application software programs located in the third layer, named application plane, that runs at the top of the control plane. This plane has a series of applications that enforce certain functions of network control, such as routing, load balancing, fault tolerance, recovery, etc. By means of a well-defined programming interface between the switches and the SDN controller, the separation of the control plane and the data plane can be understood. The controller controls the elements of the data plane directly through a well-defined Application Programming Interface (API), as shown in Figure 2, the so-called Southbound API.

SDN provides various features for all SDN-enabled devices, such as centralized and decentralized control of multiple cross-vendor network components, primarily data plane platforms with a specific abstraction layer of APIs. It decreases the difficulty of network configuration and operation achieved through the automation of high-level network feature configuration and forwarding behavior [7]. SDN enables fast implementation of new protocols and network-services leading to the high abstraction of operations. The SDN infrastructure can be tailored to the specific user application running on it through a control plane, which improves the user experience considerably.

SDN, however, has its disadvantages: the added flexibility and functionality allow additional overhead on the equipment and, as a result, processing speed and throughput capacity are forfeited. It does not mean that the overall efficiency is automatically decreasing; the SDN-enabled equipment will perform many network services and tasks performed by the end-nodes of the control layers of the network systems in a simpler and faster manner.

III. RELATED WORK

Several researches have been done in big data security and privacy, yet there is no comprehensive security architecture for big data. Because it is impossible to protect all big data and its attributes, big data security has been seen from a different perspective. Many researches and techniques have been deployed and implemented to improve big data security. Some related works are presented as the following:

In the research published in [10], an access control schemes for Hadoop data storage has been proposed based on concepts from BitTorrent and the secure sharing storage over the cloud. Their paper has described the Hadoop architecture as well as the process flows. The security risks that faced Hadoop have been reviewed and a solution for securing data stored on Hadoop over cloud systems has been proposed. This proposed solution is based on creating and distributing access token over a web server by encrypting the meta-data records from the Hadoop client and creating access token file and encrypting them as well. Finally, the encrypted access token files are distributed to the cloud storage providers. This solution has not been implemented or evaluated in terms of performance and applications for access control.

A dynamic adaptive access control scheme for Hadoop platform has been proposed in [11] that platform that adopts user suspicious status evaluation and user authorization policy based on labels and attributes. This scheme can realize the real-time dynamic adjustment of user authority according to user behavior by designing the trigger mechanism of authority automatic change, thereby more effectively protecting user sensitive information and private data in a big data environment.

A new architecture for securing MapReduce computation in the cloud has been introduced in [12] aiming to secure the Tag-MapReduce framework providing high secure MapReduce computation in the cloud with low overhead. In this paper data integrity, verification, and privacy have been focused on. Security challenges have been discussed and presented for big data processing using MapReduce. Their architecture based on a hybrid cloud and the MapReduce will move to the cloud especially the public cloud which makes it insecure. Their design not only secures the MapReduce but also considering the overhead as well as avoiding some vulnerability. A comparison between the architecture with the previous solutions has been done.

The paper published in [13] has presented a meta-model for security policies and a comprehensive framework for access management at the Infrastructure as a Service (IaaS) level. The proposed framework is being implemented on the open-source IaaS platform OpenStack, using HDFS and MySQL for data storage and adopting IBE as the encryption method. This architecture could be divided into two parts: the trusted authority domain and the data center domain. The trusted authority domain includes two components: an identity & key management engine and a policy engine. The data center domain stores the encrypted data. This paper did not include any evaluation or comparative study.

An approach to provide security to unstructured Big Data has been discussed in [14], that developed to give adequate security to the unstructured data by considering the types of the data and their sensitivity levels. They also have shown that data classification concerning sensitivity levels enhances the performance of the system.

The paper published in [15] focuses on the issue of reaching sensitive data by the cloud operators and proposes a novel approach that can efficiently split the file and separately store the data in the distributed cloud servers, in which the data cannot be directly reached by cloud service operators. The proposed scheme is entitled as Security-Aware Efficient Distributed Storage (SAEDS) model, which is mainly supported by the proposed algorithms, named Secure Efficient Data Distributions (SED2) Algorithm and Efficient Data Conflation (EDCon) Algorithm. The main problem solved by their proposed scheme is preventing cloud providers from directly reaching users' original data.

In addition, the SDN security related to big data that in the paper published in [16] security challenges in the SDN network have been addressed. They propose an approach to predict attacks in the SDN networks by applying machine learning techniques instead of using the traditional technique with threshold values, which tend to be problematic due to dynamic environments of SDN. Their proposed method not only predicts the presence of attack but also attack type by a predictive model, which represents the behaviors of the network, particularly under ARP attack, LLDP Attack, or no attack.

The research in [17] proposed a big data analysis-based secure cluster management architecture for the optimized control plane. A security authentication scheme has been also proposed for cluster management to ensure the legality of the data sources. Moreover, ant colony optimization was used to enable a big data analysis scheme and an implementation system was proposed to optimize the control plane. This work is significant in improving the performance and efficiency of applications running in SDN.

An approach to efficient network design and characterization using SDN and Hadoop has been proposed in [18], which shows a method to control characteristics and provide security to the network, which is helpful in capacity planning and attack detection and prevention and several ways.

IV. The Proposed Architecture

From the literature review, it is not clear how to have a software architecture design to present a solution for big data security. Our proposed architecture aims to secure the big data, taking into consideration the performance of writing to or reading from big data storing systems. The main two functions of this architecture are writing and reading. Many security aspects have been considered in this architecture including; file policies, fragmentation, and encryption files by using different techniques. In terms of the performance aspect, this architecture divided the load into a number of agents that will improve the performance. In addition, the data classification will improve the performance by giving each file the relative storing process with its respective importance. Finally, this architecture has flexibility because it can deal with any big data storing system. The following Figure 3 shows the proposed architecture, including the following components:

A. *Interface Agent*

This agent is responsible for displaying the Graphical User Interface (GUI) on the screen and receiving the user name and password from the user as well as displaying the file after retrieving them.

B. *Authentication*

This agent is responsible for authenticating the user and make sure only the legitimate user can enter the system. This agent checks the user name and password and uses a digital signature to confirm the identity of the user. In addition, a one-time authentication code can be used for more protection. This agent can also utilize existing authentication techniques, such as OAuth, OTP, etc.

C. Authorization

In this agent, the access rights to files will be controlled. Access control in particular is the main function of this agent. This agent displays the available files, which the user has permissions to access, read, write, etc. It is connected to policy storage that saves all file policies and user permissions. To secure this storage, the authorization agent is connected to the encryption/decryption agent to encrypt the policy storage by using public/private key cryptography. RSA algorithm will be used for this purpose. However, due to heavy computation regarding the encryption, data at rest will be encrypted and once it is not in used. Data that is being processed will only be encrypted once the related processes are terminated. In terms of giving permissions, the user can update or add permissions to his files by using this agent. However, in some cases, there is some concern regarding the access to unwanted parts of the dataset such as Personal Identifiable Information (PII) through utilizing process' global permission. In this case, all events must be logged to a log server for auditing and monitoring any incident that happened intentionally or unintentionally.

D. Main Agent

The main agent is considered as the main menu, which gives the user the ability to choose to write, update, or read files that he has the authority to access. This agent is connected to the write/update agent and read agent as well as the authorization agent.

E. Write/Update Agent

This agent is responsible for writing a new file to the system or updating existing files. It is connected to the meta-data agent to extract information about the exciting files that will be updated or to store meta-data after writing new files.

F. Read Agent

This agent is used to read files from the storing system. This agent is connected to the meta-data, which gives this agent the ability to reach the files and the needed operations if necessary. This agent also connected to the fragmentation/merge agent, which will be used in case of retrieving fragmented files. It will receive merge files from the fragmentation/merge agent and send it to the collector agent. Furthermore, it is connected to the encryption/decryption agent, which allows the read agent to retrieve encrypted files and decrypt them by using this agent and send them to the collector agent.

G. Data Classification Agent

This agent will receive the user's choice of his data and tag the files with the security classification code, which differentiate the files by its criticality. In this architecture, the data has been classified into:

1. **Sensitive Data**: The data is valuable and need the highest level of security with a different type of protection techniques. The strongest algorithms and standards will be used in this class of data to provide protection. These data might be related to national security, military secrets, or industrial secrets.
2. **Confidential Data**: this class of data has a middle level of sensitivity, needs security algorithms with good processing speed, and might use algorithms less strong than the algorithms used in the sensitive data. This class of data may include data related to military equipment, country political and economic situations, or new changes in the company's future.
3. **Public Data**: This class of data will be open for everyone or give access for registered users using id and password, such as files on the university websites given to the university students.

By using this classification, an adequate level of security will be provided and enhance the processing performance of the system.

H. Fragmentation/Merge Agent

This agent is responsible for fragmenting files into a random number of fragments with different sizes, for more protection, in terms of the writing process. In terms of the reading process, this agent is responsible for merging files and assembles the file to be complete again. This agent will be used in case of writing or updating sensitive data files. In addition, this agent is connected to the meta-data agent to add or update these files records and keep track of the files' fragments places. Also, this agent is connected to the encryption/decryption agent for encrypting these fragments.

I. Encryption/Decryption Agent

This agent will be used to encrypt confidential files as well as encrypt sensitive data that comes from the fragmentation agent. This agent is also connected to the meta-data and authorization agents to protect their storage and provide security to them. In contrast, the decryption function will be used to decrypt files and send them to the read agent as well as decrypting fragments. Finally, after encrypting the data files, the files will be sent to the storing systems.

J. Meta-Data Agent

This agent is responsible for storing all meta-data of the saved files as well as the new files. This agent is connected to five agents including; write, read, data classification, fragmentation, and encryption agents. It has meta-data storage that has been protected by using encryption algorithms.

K. Collector Agent

This agent will collect files from the storing systems and apply the reading-related functions to them and at the end sending the complete file to the interface agent.

V. EVALUATION AND COMPARATIVE STUDY

In this section, the evaluation of the proposed architecture will be discussed and compared with some related literature review. In many researches, security issues and difficulties have been discussed and many solutions have been proposed. However, a comprehensive solution for securing big data is not available yet and considered an important challenge. In addition, some researches focus on securing the big data framework, such as Hadoop, without considering a high-level abstract solution. Furthermore, the trade-off between big data security and performance has not been considered in many researches.

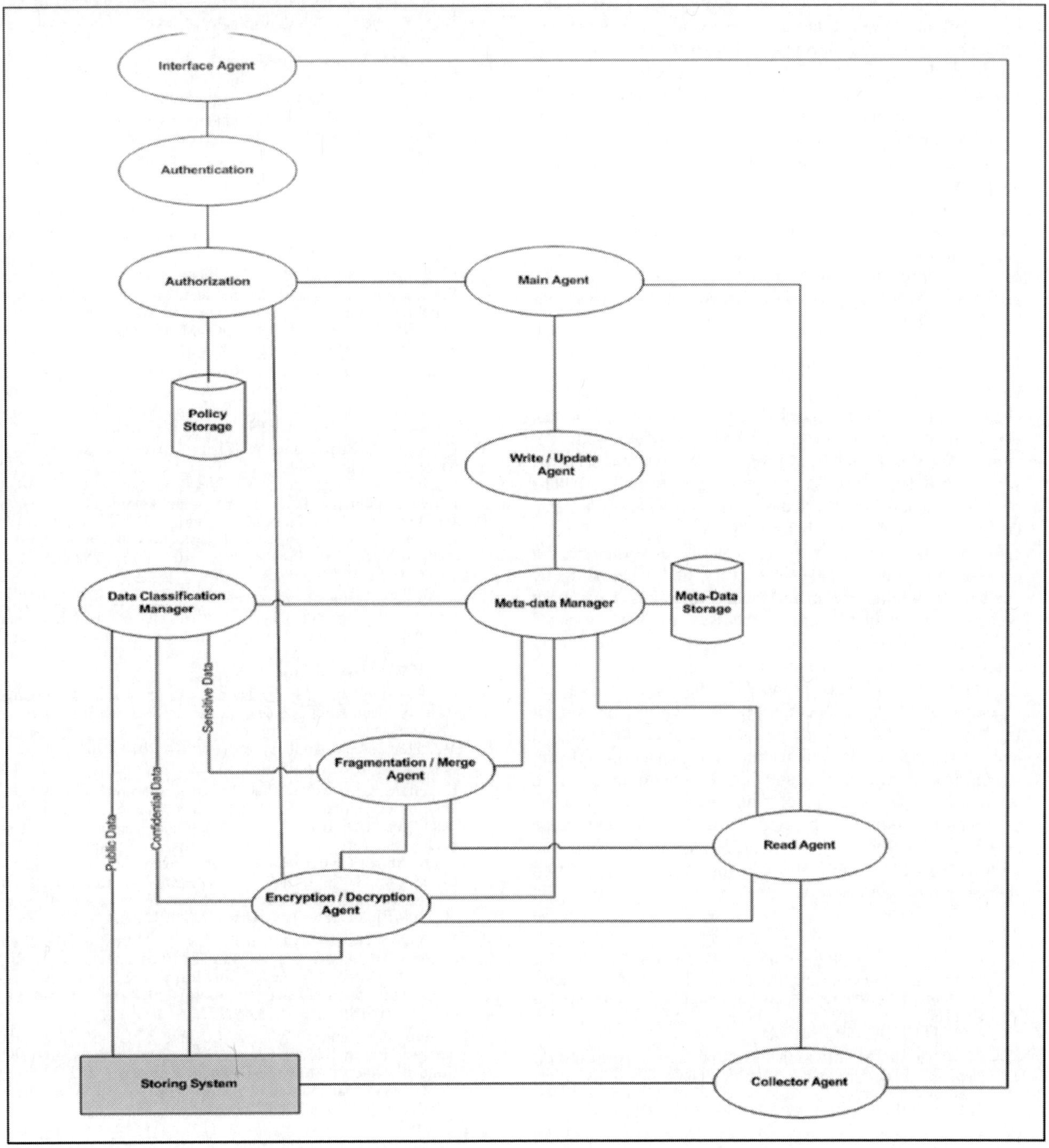

Figure 3. The Proposed Architecture

In the proposed architecture, a high-level solution has been considered, which gives this architecture the ability to work with any big data framework. This could allow this architecture to work with multiple storing systems at the same time without affecting the architecture design or functionality. In terms of performance, this architecture considered the trade-off between security and performance by classifying the data into categories and gives the proper protection to each category. This technique not only improves the performance but it saves the related resources. In addition, the load has been distributed into several agents to improve the performance, such as having the collector agent to take some load from the read agent.

The agent architecture style has been used to benefit from its advantages as well as its mobility. Dealing with a big amount of data, which is a big data characteristic, needs a mobile agent to travel rather than bring all data to the user. An agent architecture is a dynamic architecture that will be created during the runtime and has the ability to run on different software and hardware, which will be needed in a big data environment.

VI. Conclusion and Future Works

In this paper, an overview of big data and its related characteristics and security challenges have been presented. Some related works were revised and discussed. An architecture design has been proposed for big data security, which considers security and performance trade-off. The proposed architecture is based on giving each part of big data the proper security mechanism to protect it in a more efficient way. This not only improves the performance, but also saves resources and gives every part what is really needed. In addition, some sequence diagrams have been presented to explain some processes of the proposed architecture. Finally, a comparative study has been done to evaluate the proposed architecture.

For future works, the proposed architecture needs some related works to have a comprehensive security solution for big data. In addition, some performance measurements are needed to discover the architecture performance in different scenarios and to improve any notices regarding the load distributions or the processing time, especially the encryption/decryption processes and fragment/merge processes. Finally, an implementation of this architecture will be needed as well as including some transportation security solutions to improve security.

References

[1] D. S. Terzi, R. Terzi, and S. Sagiroglu, "A survey on security and privacy issues in big data," in 2015 10th International Conference for Internet Technology and Secured Transactions (ICITST), 2015, pp. 202–207, doi: 10.1109/ICITST.2015.7412089.

[2] M. Alsaeedi, M. M. Mohamad, and A. A. Al-Roubaiey, "Toward Adaptive and Scalable OpenFlow-SDN Flow Control: A Survey," IEEE Access, vol. 7, pp. 107346–107379, 2019, doi: 10.1109/ACCESS.2019.2932422.

[3] P. Adluru, S. S. Datla, and X. Zhang, "Hadoop eco system for big data security and privacy," in 2015 Long Island Systems, Applications and Technology, 2015, pp. 1–6, doi: 10.1109/LISAT.2015.7160211.

[4] Y. Gahi, M. Guennoun, and H. T. Mouftah, "Big Data Analytics: Security and privacy challenges," in 2016 IEEE Symposium on Computers and Communication (ISCC), 2016, pp. 952–957, doi: 10.1109/ISCC.2016.7543859.

[5] E. Bertino, "Big Data - Security and Privacy," in 2015 IEEE International Congress on Big Data, 2015, pp. 757–761, doi: 10.1109/BigDataCongress.2015.126.

[6] I. Gartner, "Gartner IT Glossary," 2016. [Online]. Available: http://www.gartner.com/it-glossary/big-data/. [Accessed: 01-Jul-2020].

[7] S. Mills, S. Lucas, L. Irakliotis, M. Rappa, T. Carlson, and B. Perlowitz, "Demystifying Big Data: A Practical Guide to Transforming the Business of Government," 2012.

[8] The Apache Software Foundation, "What Is Apache Hadoop?," The Apache Software Foundation, 2016. [Online]. Available: http://hadoop.apache.org/index.html. [Accessed: 01-Jul-2020].

[9] T. Das, V. Sridharan, and M. Gurusamy, "A Survey on Controller Placement in SDN," IEEE Commun. Surv. Tutorials, vol. 22, no. 1, pp. 472–503, 2020, doi: 10.1109/COMST.2019.2935453.

[10] C. Rong, Z. Quan, and A. Chakravorty, "On Access Control Schemes for Hadoop Data Storage," in 2013 International Conference on Cloud Computing and Big Data, 2013, pp. 641–645, doi: 10.1109/CLOUDCOM-ASIA.2013.82.

[11] J. Li, G. Zhao, X. Sun, and Y. Liu, "A Dynamic Adaptive Access Control Scheme for Hadoop Platform," in 2019 IEEE 2nd International Conference on Computer and Communication Engineering Technology (CCET), 2019, pp. 79–83, doi: 10.1109/CCET48361.2019.8989081.

[12] C. A. A. Bissiriou and M. Zbakh, "Towards Secure Tag-MapReduce Framework in Cloud," in 2016 IEEE 2nd International Conference on Big Data Security on Cloud (BigDataSecurity), IEEE International Conference on High Performance and Smart Computing (HPSC), and IEEE International Conference on Intelligent Data and Security (IDS), 2016, pp. 96–104, doi: 10.1109/BigDataSecurity-HPSC-IDS.2016.78.

[13] S. Li, T. Zhang, J. Gao, and Y. Park, "A Sticky Policy Framework for Big Data Security," in 2015 IEEE First International Conference on Big Data Computing Service and Applications, 2015, pp. 130–137, doi: 10.1109/BigDataService.2015.71.

[14] M. R. Islam and M. E. Islam, "An approach to provide security to unstructured Big Data," in The 8th International Conference on Software, Knowledge, Information Management and Applications (SKIMA 2014), 2014, pp. 1–5, doi: 10.1109/SKIMA.2014.7083392.

[15] K. Gai, M. Qiu, and H. Zhao, "Security-Aware Efficient Mass Distributed Storage Approach for Cloud Systems in Big Data," in 2016 IEEE 2nd International Conference on Big Data Security on Cloud (BigDataSecurity), IEEE International Conference on High Performance and Smart Computing (HPSC), and IEEE International Conference on Intelligent Data and Security (IDS), 2016, pp. 140–145, doi: 10.1109/BigDataSecurity-HPSC-IDS.2016.68.

[16] E. Unal, S. Sen-Baidya, and R. Hewett, "Towards Prediction of Security Attacks on Software Defined Networks: A Big Data Analytic Approach," in 2018 IEEE International Conference on Big Data (Big Data), 2018, pp. 4582–4588, doi: 10.1109/BigData.2018.8622524.

[17] J. Wu, M. Dong, K. Ota, J. Li, and Z. Guan, "Big Data Analysis-Based Secure Cluster Management for Optimized Control Plane in Software-Defined Networks," IEEE Trans. Netw. Serv. Manag., vol. 15, no. 1, pp. 27–38, Mar. 2018, doi: 10.1109/TNSM.2018.2799000.

[18] A. Desai, K. S. Nagegowda, and T. Ninikrishna, "Characterization Using SDN and Hadoop," 2016 Int. Conf. Circuit, Power Comput. Technol. (ICCPCT), pp. 1–6, 2016, doi: 10.1109/ICCPCT.2016.7530122.